What I Learned from God While...

GARDENING

What I Learned from God While...

GARDENING

Niki Anderson
with
Cristine Bolley

PROMISE
PRESS
An Imprint of Barbour Publishing

Be a weedexter !
Pg. 43 -

Barb
Kietzer

Published by Promise Press, an imprint of Barbour Publishing, Inc., P.O. Box 719, Uhrichsville, Ohio 44683
http://www.barbourbooks.com

 Member of the
Evangelical Christian
Publishers Association

Printed in the United States of America.

Dedicated

to a pansy—
June Marie Joyce—
who entered heaven's gardens
December 27, 1999

Contents

Editor's Preface

A Weekend Gardener

I spend three weekends each year working in my garden. My small investment of time reaps a full year of pleasure for our family and friends who often sit with us on our porch. In the spring, usually in mid-May, I plant impatiens in my shaded garden beds and experiment with full-sun annuals throughout my yard. In late fall, I exchange pansies for the impatiens and reluctantly pull the wilted annuals. Then, on Good Friday, I clear the yard of winter debris, in anticipation of an Easter egg hunt on Sunday morning.

It was during a Good Friday cleanup, not too many years ago, that I became keenly aware of the analogies the garden offered to my own experience with God. I used to rake the leaves piled in the corners of our yard, but that particular year I used the sidewalk blower that my husband uses when he mows the grass. With amazing ease, the power of the wind from the blower lifted the leaves, swept them through the gate, and into the creek bed behind our house.

I suddenly understood why the Holy Spirit is likened to the wind. We can't see Him, but we can see the work that He does. With no effort on my part, the old rotting leaves were swept away with a power much greater than my own shoulders could offer. As I worked, God continued to speak to me about the new life that was hidden beneath the soil.

Almost every event in the garden became a window into His heart. I saw another glimpse of Him at the gate and again at the creek where I knew fresh rainwater would soon come and wash old leaves away and use them to nourish new life down the stream. God's presence was strong in the garden that day, and it was evident that He enjoys winter as much as the full bloom of summer.

Winter gardens speak of promise, not loss. I was reminded that rest is an important part of growth, and stillness is an important part of learning. A prayer fell from my lips, "Lord, clean the debris away from my own overgrown, yet seemingly dormant life."

It had been my belief that we need to do great things for God, but He has consistently shown me that He wants us to simply enjoy the great things He has done for us. Yes, God gave Adam work to do in the garden, but it was also His idea to just walk together in the cool of the evening, and take a whole day off each week.

Thus, the idea was birthed for a series of books written by individuals who have experienced God while enjoying their lives. The idea was fresh in my heart when I first met Niki Anderson at a writer's conference in Idaho where we were both teaching classes. I told her I was looking for stories that would illustrate God's desire to participate in our special interests, such as a person's love for cats. She quickly responded, "I could write that book! I've learned so much about God while watching the cats He created."

Her award-winning devotional book quickly became a best-seller, reaching thousands upon thousands of cat lovers. When she said, "Oh, I garden, too," I knew that I had found the writer for another favorite pastime where God could be found.

After reading Niki's stories, I was eager to do my spring planting this year. While transplanting seedlings from last year's periwinkle, I thought of her story, "Exemplar Volunteers." Now when I look at the seedlings, I will think of volunteering my time just for the joy of being involved. The story "Naturalizing" gave me the courage to invest in an unusual mix of colorful perennials for a bed that had previously left me unsatisfied. It is now filled with purple crepe myrtle, bright yellow daylilies, blue salvia, and bordered with deep violet petunias. My family voted it as their favorite part of the garden this year.

I'm also keeping a gardening journal now, as Niki suggests. The first entry captures my own lessons learned from God while gardening. Then I list the special features of each new planting and record the feeding and watering instructions that came with the plant. A section called "Wildlife" gives a summary of my interaction with the birds, mice, snakes, rabbits, and bugs that live in my garden. . .but that will be another book. I encourage you to keep a diary of what you learn from God while gardening; I'm sure you will be pleasantly surprised.

CRISTINE BOLLEY

Acknowledgments

I am indebted to many old and new friends who told their stories or gave me leads. Those who shared their accounts are usually named in their stories. Others, who were not key characters in the stories, were primary sources. Those named below are worthy of mention (groups of names listed alphabetically):

- Susan Keyes, Director of Providence Center for Faith and Healing for "Garden Medicine Nourishes Faith"; Debbie Clem, Katherine Cole, Lynn Mandyke, Sally Reynolds, and Linda Yeomans for "Garden Restoration"; Karen Wingate for "Firstfruit Felicitations"; Christine Harder Tangvald for "Forever-greens"; Dr. Peter Gail for facts in "Weed Eaters."

- Also, my husband, Bob, for his abiding patience and love, Ruth Danner for her keen critique, Michael Williams for his brotherly encouragement, local librarians for their willing assistance, and Cris Bolley for her contribution to my books in the hobby series.

- To all of you, I offer sincere thanks.

Author's Introduction

Welcome to My Garden

Whether a garden is an acre of vegetables, a small yard of flower beds, or a potted herb on the windowsill, each one rewards us with its growth. Like our gardens, we, too, must be ever growing in the seed rows of life. Lessons found in the garden give us rich instruction. While reading these tales about statuesque iris, a brilliant orange pepper, or a smiling pansy, you will learn about generosity, kindness, and hope. Fifty themes will be planted in your heart.

A few extras complement each story. The opening Bible verse is like the garden gate. Swing wide your heart's entrance as you read what God says. Then ponder the kernel of truth contained in His Word.

A true story follows. You'll be enchanted by a historic garden, a cat garden, and a rose garden; you'll be inspired by a greenhouse garden, a lost garden, and a peony garden. And you'll harvest truth from a sunken garden, a preacher's garden, and a weed garden!

"The Root of the Matter" summarizes and highlights the fundamental truth in each story. Let it take root in your life.

"The Fragrance of Praise" is your opportunity to offer God the sweet scent of gratefulness. Each prayer expresses gratitude for a garden truth. Take a moment to praise the Master Gardener.

To assist your green thumb, you'll need a wheelbarrow of "Garden Tools." Don't overlook these helpful tips. Topics range from garden web sites and pruning guides to bulb types and garden signs.

Finally, in "Wildflowers" you'll find a colorful and random scattering of facts, poems, quotations, statistics, and humorous anecdotes. May they delight you along the roadsides of life.

Compiled herein, I offer you the shoots of wisdom, the sprouts of joy, and the blades of wonder I have discovered while learning from God in the garden. May each beautiful truth encourage you to grow.

NIKI ANDERSON

Fair-Weather Gardener

Remember: sparse sowing, sparse reaping;
sow bountifully, and you will reap bountifully.
2 CORINTHIANS 9:6 NEB

For years I reveled in the pageantry of color-crayon tulips, dainty crocuses, and bicolor daffodils brightening the gray landscape around town. As my husband and I drove through our community, I would point and exclaim, "Oh, honey, look at the pink tulips! And over there! Did you see the sweet circle of crocuses at the base of that fountain? Isn't it charming?"

I waxed eloquent. "Tulips are the cheeriest testimony to spring, aren't they? They herald the end of cold and the Passion of Easter;

they're such a gala prelude to summer." Graciously, he refrained from the most natural reply: Then why don't you plant some?

Year after year, I admired the glories of bulbous beauties bursting forth in the yards of my neighbors, in flower beds by the church doors, in window boxes at the florists'—everywhere but in my yard, where no bulbs were wakening. And just as punctual as spring, I would again resolve to plant bulbs in October—"for sure this year."

Finally determined, my daughter and I went tulip shopping one fall. Like four-year-olds loose in a candy store, we plucked varieties from nearly every bin in the aisle—the early flowering, the midseason flowering, the late flowering, the lacy, and the typical. Our tight fists gripped bags and bags of bulbs.

"Thirty-two dollars and seventy-eight cents, please," said the cashier. *Whoa,* I thought. *That's a lot of tulips!* But home we went like two little Dutch girls.

I wish I could say we set all seventy-some bulbs into wintertime beds. But Jodie was facing a new quarter at college and I was facing my annual archenemy—the chill of fall temperatures. This warm-weather gardener does not mind sweat or heat rash, but she hates the cold that accompanies late fall duty. That year, as usual, indoor activities seized my time, and the bulbs rotted in the basement. In spring I chided myself once more, "If only I had planted."

Several seasons have passed since I've become routine about fall planting. My yard is now host to crocuses, tulips, anemones, and narcissus. Each year their blooms remind me of the basic premise of gardening and of life—I reap only what I sow. No bulbs, no gladiolus. Likewise, I must write letters if I want to receive them, speak encouragingly, give generously, listen attentively, and offer praise enthusiastically if I expect the same in return.

The plant kingdom waits only to be planted. And kindnesses, like plants, also produce a harvest—if I plant goodness, it will spring up later in my own garden!

The Root of the Matter: Believing something to be true is
    not the same as acting on truth. Jesus said, "Now that
    you know these things, you will be blessed if you do
    them" (John 13:17). The lesson from my rotting bulbs
    is a good example of what Jesus' disciple, James, must
    have meant when he wrote, "faith by itself, if it is not
    accompanied by action, is dead. . . . I will show you

my faith by what I do" (James 2:17–18). The more bulbs I plant in the fall, the more blooms I will have in my spring garden. The more I do what God commands, the more fruit He will produce in my life.

The Fragrance of Praise: Thank You, God, for the cold seasons that give repose to earthbound sleepers and grant gardeners time to reflect.

Garden Tools: After digging up bulbs, allow them to dry out for a week or more before putting them in storage. Shake them in bulb dust to prevent storage rot. Until time to replant, keep them in a dry spot where temperatures remain under 60 degrees.

Wildflowers: Many popularly named bulbs are among one of the five bulblike perennial plants: corms (crocus), rhizomes (iris), true bulbs (onion and daffodil), tubers (begonias), and root tubers (dahlia). Use the height of the bulb as a guide, and plant the bulb three to five times deeper than its height.

Exemplar Volunteers

Serve the LORD with gladness.
PSALM 100:2

Do perennials survive the winter or am I thinking of annuals?" Though I had asked that question numerous times, I could never remember the difference. Gardening lingo was not familiar to me. Neither my parents nor grandparents were serious gardeners. Mom used to joke about her monochrome thumb–it was perpetually pink. "I can't keep anything alive!" she admitted to her green-thumbed friends. Monthly, Mom listed sugar, rice, potatoes, and "new plant" on her grocery list of staples. Potted flowers filled her grocery cart almost as often as cake flour.

When still a novice myself in the garden kingdom, I was perplexed by other words besides perennial and annual. Another mysterious term entered my conversations with gardeners—the word *volunteer*. "Poppies aren't perennials, but they will volunteer," commented a garden guru. *Volunteer? What does that mean?* I wondered. I learned as much by asking questions—and exposing my ignorance—as I did by panning through garden books.

"A volunteer is an annual that reseeds itself in the spring," a neighbor explained one day. How ingratiating that these willing annuals simply cast their seeds to the moist, warm earth and begin a new round of growth. I am spared! No knees sunk in the dirt, no seed rows to dig.

I like the concept of a volunteer. I've met this noble species at church, at thrift stores, through meals-on-wheels, but I never imagined I could grow them in my backyard! My perception of these types are people with natural stamina and solid stature. The gentle designs of calendula and forget-me-nots hardly fit my stereotype. I find it comical that kitten-face pansies and ruffled marigolds are members of this company called volunteers.

Some of the most important people in my life have been volunteers—those who brought meals to the house when my husband was hospitalized, friends who worked the kitchen at my daughter's wedding, and the neighbor who helps my husband carry heavy tools from car to workshop. What would hospitals do without student volun-TEENS, and how would inner-city shelters continue without volunteer cooks and servers? Habitat for Humanity, which builds houses for low-income families, is another organization facilitated by nonconscripted helpers. Countless operations around the world are aided by those who offer themselves without expectation of wage or compensation.

In whatever way you are qualified to best volunteer, why not seed yourself in some nearby soil, take root, and start budding? I recall the line in an old hymn, "Will you be enlisted as a volunteer? Will you answer quickly with a ready cheer?" I hope I will answer "yes"–as cheerily as an orange poppy in full bloom.

The Root of the Matter: The difference between hirelings and volunteers is their motivation. The hireling is paid in gold. The volunteer is a soldier of love.

The Fragrance of Praise: We are grateful, God, for the unselfish service of volunteers among our families and friends, in religious orders, and in numerous charitable organizations.

Garden Tools: Though reseeding annuals spare the gardener the effort of planting, the wind may carry volunteer seeds to far areas of the garden. Simply uproot young starts and discard or transplant them in a bed of your choice.

Wildflowers: Handheld bouquets called tussie-mussies were a Victorian tradition. Sent in lieu of a written note, each nosegay communicated a message in the language of flowers. For example, a get-well tussie-mussie might contain plumbago (antidote), a rose (love), feverfew (good health), and pussy willow (recovery from illness).

Best Garden, Best Neighbor

"Love your neighbor as yourself."
LUKE 10:27

Not all gardeners qualify as best neighbors, but Erika Vathis won the "Good Neighbor of the Year" title among 149 contestants on the south side of Spokane, Washington. For over twenty years, I had driven past her house. The floral display during blooming seasons always pleased and intrigued me. When I visited her for an interview, I learned this ardent gardener was also a warm and cordial person.

I was a stranger in her driveway when she happened outdoors. Her welcoming smile was as inviting as the clematis, forsythia, tulips, snowdrops, holly, crocus, and numerous other plants artfully and seasonally spaced everywhere I glanced.

A city girl who grew up in Berlin, Erika wanted a garden soon after she married. She and her husband were living in Arizona, and he was about to retire from thirty-five years of service in the foreign embassy. "I want to live where there are four seasons," she told him. Zone five in the Pacific Northwest met those criteria.

Erika has cultivated their residential lot for thirty years with a prize-winning garden of fruit-bearing cherry, pear, apple, apricot, and plum trees; blackberries, strawberries, and blueberries; squash, kohlrabi, peas, beans, tomatoes, corn, potatoes; and annuals, roses, perennials, and ornamentals. Stone walkways shaped like flowers with long stepping-stone stems guide visitors through her garden. A gazebo provides support for climbers, like her butterfly bush and trumpet vine, and a pergola is adorned with berry vines. An electric fountain gurgles in the summer, and nearby a large barrel collects rainwater that Erika describes as "God's gift from heaven." She totes the chlorine-free water to many of her plants.

I asked her if she was in a garden club. She answered in her delightful German accent, "No, no; I have no time with a garden to tend." But her reputation is well-known in area garden clubs and has earned her recognition even in *Sunset* magazine.

In the summer, Erika shares her bounty by delivering fruit,

vegetables, and bouquets to her neighbors. She cans and freezes the surplus edibles.

Erika's neighborliness goes beyond sharing her harvest. One neighbor, Melody Chestnut, submitted this testimony for the Good Neighbor Contest: "Erika is always there if you need your mail picked up or your house watched while on vacation. (She) helps many of the. . .elderly people in the area by walking with them, running little errands, and taking them goodies. (She) walks some people's dogs and once even helped me raise some orphaned baby squirrels. Whenever it snows, Erika shovels anyone's walk who isn't able to do his or her own and does it all winter—not just once or twice. She always waves and has a friendly smile for everyone. No one has a better neighbor."

Meeting someone like Erika is a double inspiration—I'm challenged to be a better neighbor as well as a better gardener!

The Root of the Matter: Erika enjoys the best part of gardening; she sows kindness and reaps the love of her neighbors. Jesus said, " 'Give, and it will be given to you. A good measure, pressed down, shaken together and running over, will be poured into your lap. For with the measure you use, it will be measured to you' " (Luke 6:38 NIV).

The Fragrance of Praise: Thank You, God, for those who excel at their hobbies but still take time for people nearby.

Garden Tools: Save your knees! Purchase a couple of kneeling mats to cushion your skin from the abrasion of soil and pebbles. Spare your overalls unnecessary wear from grit and mud with a buffer between you and the ground.

Wildflowers: "The impersonal hand of government can never replace the helping hand of a neighbor."

HUBERT H. HUMPHREY

Roses, Roses, Roses

The desert shall rejoice, and blossom as the rose.
ISAIAH 35:1

When a single working woman, Wendy Burton, moved into a two-story Victorian house with a large yard, the neighbors sighed. "Watch that place go downhill now!" But much to their delight, all summer they noticed strangers stop to photograph the twice-painted, tidy home with its scalloped flower beds filled with an extravaganza of ninety-four rosebushes—Wendy planted ninety-three of them!

The day of my visit I felt myself smile as I approached the house. The white picket fence, flowered walkway, big porch with wicker chairs, potted flowers, and antique trunk spoke to me of yesteryear.

Wendy invited me into the foyer where I saw the first display of her indoor flowers–gangly geranium stems dangled over the sides of a Red Flyer wagon. I admired the stairway to the right and French doors to the left. A glance into the living room revealed antique furniture that matched the old-fashioned cabbage roses brushing against windows and siding outside.

"My Irish grandparents were farmers, and my parents also loved to garden," said Wendy. Not surprisingly, green is her favorite color, but the rose is her favorite flower. Her fascination with roses was born the day she watched her minister-father cut a single rose from the family garden–dewdrops clinging to its petals–and give it to her mother.

There's a faith-stirring story behind Wendy's home and gardens. Eight years ago, she was suddenly single, jobless, and homeless. "You've promised to provide, God," she prayed. "Have at it!" Within two months, God provided her with a mortgage to assume and a business she could afford–with $500 to spare! "It was only later I realized this house and yard were in every detail what I'd never been bold enough to pray for; and the consignment clothing store I purchased was the sort of venture I'd always wanted to try." Teary-eyed, she said, "It's a constant reminder of God's faithfulness.

"Sharing my roses is how I've turned that once-barren time of my life into a blessing for others." Like the day she gave five visiting college students each a bouquet for their mothers. One time a woman stopped on the sidewalk to revel in the garden view and commented, "My mother loved lavender." Wendy promptly picked a handful to give the mother who lived in a retirement home nearby. In summer, Wendy's business counters are graced with her bouquets, usually arranged in quaint containers. Acquaintances who are hospitalized and countless others receive Wendy's flowers.

She showed me a large basketful of potpourri–hundreds of rose petals mixed with sweet William, bee balm, and other picks. "I plan to make rosewater body splash this year, and because I employ ladybugs rather than pesticides, this fall I'll make rose hip tea."

In Old English flower vocabulary, the cabbage rose means "ambassador of love." Both Wendy and her roses are truly envoys of love–multiplied times ninety-four!

The Root of the Matter: God is in the business of restoring lives. As we draw near to Him, our homes and gardens reflect the glory of His presence. Wouldn't it be nice if everyone in the neighborhood would take their heartbreaks to the Lord and exchange them for roses?

The Fragrance of Praise: Dear God, I thank You for growing beautiful things from the soil of depleted lives.

Garden Tools: The centifolia roses are often called cabbage roses because their whorled petals and lush, rounded blossoms resemble cabbage heads.

Wildflowers: The dog rose was so named because it was believed the root could cure the bites of mad dogs. A dog-bitten Roman soldier of the Praetorian guard was purportedly cured of hydrophobia by eating the root.

Just a Farmer's Daughter

Train a child in the way he should go,
and when he is old he will not turn from it.
PROVERBS 22:6 NIV

No one ever likes to leave home." Joan aimed her comment at a clump of snowdrops she was uprooting. Experiencing transplant is something she understands well. She remembers leaving home for boarding school at age seven. Years later, the widow and her son left the Norfolk Broads in England and sailed to America where she has lived since 1963.

Joan grew up on an Elizabethan estate ("Eliz-a-BEE-than," her British pronunciation). Stokesby Hall, over five hundred years old, was previously owned by Sir Nicholas Dagworth, uncle of the beheaded queen, Anne Boleyn. The estate's brick front was inset with family crests. The face of the home was draped with lavender wisteria reaching three stories to the roof. Adam, one of the famed architects for St. Paul's Cathedral, designed the front door. Half of the thousand acres surrounding the estate was grazing land; the rest was fields of wheat, barley, and sugar beets. Though raised in an upper-class family, Joan said, "I was just a farmer's daughter."

Gardens bedecked the estate in a panoply of designs and color. Two gardeners tended the Blue Walk, a ten-foot pathway of blue flowers; a vegetable garden; a sunken garden; and both a rock and water garden. The knot garden, low sculpted hedges in interlacing bands and patterns enclosing colorful plants, was viewed at best vantage from a window above. Breakfast was served during warm months near a garden that encircled a courtyard outside the dining room. Two tennis courts were in view of cattle and Suffolk horses. The animals were separated from tennis players by the "ha-ha"—a ten-foot brick wall at the bottom of a slope. Joan smiled as she reminisced. "Beyond an iron gate, our driveway wound between narcissus and larger daffodils, and lime trees that perfumed the drive."

Joan's memories of the English gardens nurtured her dream to replicate them on her "postage-stamp lot" in America. But working as a secretary and raising a son left little time to garden. Upon retirement, she began in earnest.

Her flamingo bed is an oval shape of evenly spaced pink tulips rising from a sea of blue forget-me-nots. She also grows specialties from other countries like Swiss gentians and English wallflowers. Her roses include miniatures, a centerpiece David Austin floribunda, and garage-high climbing roses intertwined with earlier blooming pink honeysuckle or double-blooming clematis. A pond encloses a rock garden, which hosts alpines of pincushion flower, lungwort, sedum, rock thyme, pink cranesbill, *Dianthus plumarius,* and white and blue bellflowers, among others. A white spiraea hedge borders her largest bed, which is a collection of perennials.

Besides gardening, Joan walks six miles with her hiking club once a week. What a lady! Maybe I should have aspired to be "just a farmer's daughter."

The Root of the Matter: Our upbringing roots us in the
principles, traditions, and affections of our heritage.
Gardens were a hallmark at the estate where Joan

grew up. She beheld their beauty and inhaled their heady aromas. The passing of many years never diminished her desire for gardens. Though her dream was long delayed, her heritage at last found root in her own backyard.

The Fragrance of Praise: Thank You, God, for my birthright—the good gifts of my family legacy.

Garden Tools: Memorialize your family by planting something in your garden to honor them.

Wildflowers: "The love of gardening is a seed that once sown never dies."

GERTRUDE JEKYLL,
British horticulturist and author

Buried Treasure

I will give you the treasures of darkness,
riches stored in secret places,
so that you may know that I am the LORD.
ISAIAH 45:3 NIV

It's an ample house with lovely big windows, Bill." Laurie was hopeful.

Though previously condemned, the house had been improved enough to barely meet federal codes. The Kleins purchased the neighborhood eyesore with plans to restore it.

The previous owner, a fence contractor, had been lackadaisical about disposing of his surplus concrete and other collections. Rusty nails, broken glass, outdated hardware, and chunks of concrete were disguised in shoulder-high grass.

Cleanup began while an elderly neighbor watched with relief and delight. Pickup trucks hauled away debris that Alice had been forced to view from her well-kept garden. One day she arrived at Laurie's doorstep. "Welcome! Here are some hyacinth bulbs. You'll love their scent and beauty."

Laurie was both touched and stupefied. She didn't know which side of the bulb was up—or down! Laurie had not learned the art that grandmother, mother, and sister had practiced passionately. Thankful for Alice's offer to supervise, she planted her first bulbs. Alice was capable of answering any question about vegetable, flower, or herb. Thus, she became both garden mentor and dear friend.

Her first recommendation was compost. Laurie hammered holes into a garbage can and layered sand, soil, clippings, eggshells, coffee grounds, bonemeal, and worms inside the container. The conglomeration was difficult to stir and produced only a small amount of black gold in return for a large amount of effort.

Soon the garbage can was replaced with an unconfined, neglected pile. As the Kleins' newborn took priority over composting, the pile became nothing more than a spot where Bill dumped grass clippings.

One day after a spell of yardwork and a hot shower, Bill noticed his wedding band was missing. Heartsick, he presumed it was lost down the drain. But he and Laurie continued to search without success. Their matching rings had been sculpted with symbols of intimate meaning—a treble clef, a moon, an ocean, and a heart. Replacing it with something inferior in sentiment was unthinkable. They finally resigned themselves to their loss.

With additions of fallen branches and other waste, the compost pile grew from a tidy mass to a towering heap. Two years later, Bill decided to clear the mountain. A rich loamy product had fermented at the bottom. Hooray! Bill loaded the rich mixture into buckets.

A clink against his shovel interrupted the quiet job. "What's that?" he said aloud. *Probably more salvage,* he figured. Curious, he stooped and ran his fingers through the soil. Buried in the blended waste was his wedding ring! "Laurie!" he shouted. It was a day of hugging, laughter, and gratefulness.

The Root of the Matter: How like God to conceal treasures in unlikely places. A condemned piece of property became the birthplace for a friendship and a garden; a pile of compost became a treasure chest for a token of love.

The Fragrance of Praise: Thank You, God, for Your everywhere presence and Your everyday surprises.

Garden Tools: Learn the difference between various soil amendments. Compost, composted manure, humus, topsoil, and peat moss are a few.

Wildflowers: During childhood, Laurie's favorite book was *The Secret Garden.* When she became a mother, she cut a path to a secret garden in a corner of her yard. The flowered hideaway was a gift to her daughters.

Weed Eaters

Then God said,
"I give you every seed-bearing plant on
the face of the whole earth and
every tree that has fruit with seed in it.
They will be yours for food."
GENESIS 1:29 NIV

Like mother, like daughter," it's said. How true for daughter Barb Kietzer, who inherited her mother's savor for dandelions. Unlike the typical gardener, Barb doesn't share the common notion that all weeds are bad.

Barb remembers a springtime routine in her childhood when

she lived on a small farm in southwestern Michigan. She would follow her mother into their gardens and watch her select choice dandelions. "Mother carried a large pan and a knife, stopping to cut only greens that met her strict requirements—no buds, no flowers." Dandelions are unpleasantly strong if picked after they flower. Young, elongated leaves are best.

"When Mother's pan was full, we would head home, empty the greens in the kitchen sink, and wash them in salted water. The crisp dandelions were then put in a plastic bag and placed in the refrigerator until time to prepare the salad," Barb recounts.

Later that day, the smell of sizzling bacon would fill the house. "Mother would fry three or four slices. To a few teaspoons of the bacon fat, she added equal amounts of water, cider vinegar, and sugar, stirring until the sugar was dissolved. Mother filled a colorful pottery bowl with chopped raw greens, over which she poured the hot dressing mixed with crumbled bacon. We dove in! Those salads were equal to homemade ice cream," she recalls. "We competed to see which of us could eat the biggest serving of the deep green leaves."

Now retired, Barb still emulates her mother's relish for dandelions. Throughout her adulthood, she has grown dandelions in raised beds alongside her cherry tomatoes. She has a Dandy-lion

Pizza recipe ready to enter in the 2000 National Dandelion Cook-Off contest.

"As far back as I can remember, I've enjoyed experimenting with recipes," she said. Her recipe for Strawberry Muffin Cones was published in the national magazine, *Taste of Home.* She bakes and sells twenty dozen cookies weekly and donates the proceeds to animal shelters. She's been featured as "Cook of the Week" in her local newspaper. One ingredient in her Longevity Muffins is, of course, more greens (spinach)!

Webster defines a weed as a plant that is not wanted where it is growing. By that definition, Barb and her mother would never categorize a dandelion as a weed. The Latin name for dandelion is translated "official remedy for disorders." Trace minerals in colloidal form and in sufficient concentrations to support optimal health reside in dandelions. This nutritious food is generally devalued.

The Root of the Matter: A weed is a weed only in the opinion of the beholder. I wonder how often we misjudge values? Perhaps we would benefit if we ignored commonly accepted opinions and placed value on every created thing. God made nothing without purpose. May we be particularly careful to value all human beings, those whom God values so highly that He calls them His children!

The Fragrance of Praise: Creator of all vegetation, thank You for Your liberality.

Garden Tools: Check out this web site on edible weeds: http://www.goosefootacres.com

Wildflowers: Nutrients in dandelions include beta-carotene (more than carrots), potassium (more than bananas), lecithin (more than soybeans), iron (more than spinach), and vitamins A, C, E, thiamin, riboflavin, calcium, phosphorus, and magnesium!

Name-Calling of the Fondest Sort

*You will be called by a new name that
the mouth of the LORD will bestow.*
ISAIAH 62:2 NIV

Can you tell me if you carry Mrs. Johnson plants?" asked a customer.

Dahlores hesitated. Though her plant knowledge spanned thirty years as a florist and eighteen years as an employee at Stanek's Nursery, this plant name was new. There was no such cultivar displayed on the racks, and none of her catalogs listed a Mrs. Johnson plant.

Dahlores skewed her eyebrows. "Can you describe it?"

"It grows in a mound and blooms in spring with tiny golden flowers in dense clusters; the leaves are grayish-green. Mom planted it in our rock garden and in borders."

This was not the first time someone asked Dahlores for a plant by neither its botanical nor common name. "It sounds like basket-of-gold," said Dahlores. "Did your mother have a friend or neighbor named Johnson who may have given her a start of the plant?"

"Why, yes! Mrs. Johnson lived down the street, and hers was the garden of everyone's envy. I bet Mom got the first clump from her! I never made the connection, though we always called it 'Mrs. Johnson plant.'" The happy customer left with a whole flat, but Dahlores doubts the buyer will ever call her plants basket-of-gold.

Dahlores tells a similar story about the Hartsungs, homesteaders who lived next door to the nursery. The Hartsungs had an apple tree whose pulp was soft pink. Nursery employees marveled at the rosy pulp and asked repeatedly, "What kind of apple tree is that?"

The answer was always the same. "It's the 'Missouri Methodist pink applesauce tree!'" Transplanted from Missouri, it grew on the property of the Methodist church. When Mrs. Hartsung harvested the apples she always made pink applesauce.

Dahlores understands the origination of such names. "For several generations people have named plants after the person who shared a shoot, a start, or a clump of overgrowth." The "Farmer Wilson Shrub," or "the Widow's Flower," or "Nancy's Vine" would not be listed in a horticulture manual. Each was named after someone who passed it on. The next person to accept a start would likely rename it after the new giver.

Personalizing names of plants by other associations is also common. A weed that Dahlores's father called the Outhouse Flower was a pretty bloomer that grew somewhere you'd probably suspect—around the outhouse. Her grandmother's deep violet iris smelled just like grape juice. When Dahlores was a little girl she called the rare bearded iris the Grape Juice Flower.

The Root of the Matter: Though we teach our children that name-calling is wrong, plant names such as these are assigned with the fondest of intent. Don't be offended if the rare *Helleborus* you shared with a relative now bears your name. Consider yourself flattered. You have been endeared in someone's heart and in someone's garden.

The Fragrance of Praise: O God, I praise Your name above all others.

Garden Tools: Invest in at least one garden volume that contains an index with a cross-reference of botanical and common names.

Wildflowers: A century ago, a vessel called a *vasculum* was used by naturalists and even children for collecting botanical specimens from the wild. The small tin cylinder with latching lid and canvas or leather shoulder strap was gaily lithographed or painted and had one or two compartments.

The Gardener's Presence

God is our refuge and strength,
an ever-present help in trouble.
PSALM 46:1 NIV

I f only I'd taken a few minutes to inspect the garden," I up-braided myself after finding the leaves of my London pride chewed by root weevils. The previous week I had been busy—too absorbed to take even a five-minute stroll through my garden. Neglect always has consequences.

The most critical advice gardeners should heed is that of being regularly present—to observe and prevent, to notice and nourish, to pull a weed, treat a disease, or in scores of other ways, to supervise the life over which God has made us a steward.

We practice constancy in the oversight of our children and our businesses but wonder why a garden suffers when we give it only erratic attention. Seedlings die because we skipped two days of watering when they were still young and frail. Moss overtook an area due to excessive watering. Why didn't I turn off the sprinkler system that week it rained?

Monitoring the dynamics in our gardens is mandatory for its health. Sporadic regard pays in sick, starved, dehydrated, or struggling plants. We may need to trim a ground cover before it spreads to the grass and becomes a great effort to uproot later. Unless we're consistently examining the activity in our garden, problems get out of hand, and through negligence, we become responsible for the demise of our green residents.

Being present is a basic statute. Before I learned this hard lesson, nowhere had I seen a chapter in a garden text that read, "Rule Number One—Be There!" Though books implied this rule, nothing taught me as plainly or convincingly as my experience. I've discovered the promise, "I'll be there for you," is applicable to both gardens and relationships. This fact is so fundamental, that when you leave for a vacation or a business trip, you might consider hiring a garden-sitter. Ask someone knowledgeable. A sudden infestation of aphids may require a pesticide, or an unexpected siege of hot days will demand extra watering. The solutions are easy, but if we are not present to heed the need, we can't be good caretakers.

Be a circumspect gardener. Stay in touch with your garden if you expect it to prosper.

The Root of the Matter: I find this principle so like my relationship with God. If I'm too busy to read His Word or to wait prayerfully in His presence, I may not realize I'm getting dry, or I've become diseased by a pestilent attitude, or am in need of extra water due to a fiery trial. God's always there for me, but if I don't place myself in His presence, I won't notice His signs, hear His voice, or respond to His instructions. I must be consistently related to God if I hope to grow.

The Fragrance of Praise: Thank You, God, for the dependability of Your presence.

Garden Tools: Black circles surrounded by yellow rings
characterize black spot, a fungus that disfigures rose
leaves and weakens the plant. Spraying every four
days with a solution of baking soda (one tablespoon
soda to one gallon water) helps prevent black spot.

Wildflowers: "The most important thing you can put in the
garden is your own shadow."

AUTHOR UNKNOWN

Wild About Wildflowers

We have put our hope in the living God,
who is the Savior of all men.
1 TIMOTHY 4:10 NIV

The vase was a water bottle and the flower was a single butter-cup. As happy as though my husband had extended a dozen roses, I smiled coyly and kissed his sweaty cheek. Each year Bob makes his first bike trek over a bluff two miles from our home. In spring, the hillside is alive with wildflowers in shades of yellow, lavender, and white. Though it's become Bob's tradition to bring me one tiny flower after that first ride of the season, I never remember until he pours a floating bloom onto his palm and says, "For you."

It's a moment of love.

My earliest memories of wildflowers date back to hikes with my big brother; he was ten and I was six. He held my hand as we crossed San Benancio Road in Salinas, California, and then wiggled under a fence and began our climb to the hilltop. There we were met by swathes of orange poppies I will never forget. We always came home with a bouquet for Mom. Our gift of flowers was a moment of love.

The sweetest story of wildflower love is the one I heard from Patsy Johnson. Her seven-year-old daughter, Shannon, took an interest in wildflowers when she began chemotherapy treatments for leukemia.

Patsy and Shannon's passion for wildflowers led them on many walks and frequent journeys around the Great Lakes. Their searches prompted "field trips" even along the shoulders of the New York interstate highway. Shannon's sister remembers well. "Mom would holler, 'Look! Wildflowers! Let's go see!' " Patsy would swerve to a stop, and Shannon and her mother would spring from the car to retrieve a specimen. They would compare the flower with the key in their guidebook and happily identify another sample.

Soon, Shannon became more proficient than Patsy at remembering the names of wildflowers. "Our fascination led us to in-depth studies," she said. "We learned about medicinal values and how earlier cultures, often the Indians, treated diseases with curative varieties. Food value was also something we investigated." It was a joyful diversion at a time when both mother and daughter needed a focus beyond the gravity of Shannon's illness.

Poignant wildflower hunts concluded sadly when Shannon succumbed at last to her disease. Patsy took many solitary walks through woods and meadows after Shannon's death, reliving the wildflower hunts with her daughter. She found great solace in memories of their shared hobby. "I've often surmised that if Shannon had lived she might have become a botanist," said Patsy. "She never tired of our quests for new flowers."

The Root of the Matter: Wildflowers are particularly skilled
at rendering moments of love, perhaps because they
are much like their Creator. God's love is wildly lavish
and everywhere present. It surprises us at the bend of
a trail, in a field where we didn't expect it, or beside a
freeway on a busy day. The greatest display of God's

love was when God sent His Son to the world and granted us a Savior from our sins. Wild about wild-flowers? Let's also fall wildly in love with the Savior.

The Fragrance of Praise: Thank You, dear God, for Your astounding love.

Garden Tools: Always obtain permission before picking wildflowers. Buy wildflower plants at the nursery. Because woodland wildflowers mature very slowly, they are expensive.

Wildflowers: Wildflowers dot meadow grasses in colors like "confetti from a child's garden party."

Souvenirs,
Gifts from the Garden

Collectibles

The grass withers, the flower fades,
But the word of our God stands forever.
ISAIAH 40:8 NKJV

It's an heirloom." I've heard the designation all my life. Mom was an antique collector, and many things in our home were inherited—like the pendulum clock that traveled west with my grandmother aboard a covered wagon. But when a gardener sits beside the vegetable plot with salt shaker in hand, eating a warm, ripe tomato, I don't expect to hear the tomato referred to as an heirloom.

Lifelong gardeners are intrigued with the current trend to rescue plants from the past. There may never be another mantel clock like my grandmother's, and there may never be another tomato like the ones she grew. Antique clocks and heirloom seeds must be saved. Among the varieties of vegetables listed in a U.S. Department of Agriculture commercial seed inventory in 1903, only 3 percent survive today.

Heirloom vegetables and flowers are varieties that are passed down from generation to generation by propagation of their seeds. Heirlooms duplicate the parent plants, whereas hybrids are first-generation offspring of two different varieties that might not be able to duplicate themselves. The benefits of heirlooms are multifaceted. Besides their unique flavors and fragrances, they tend to be hardy and have greater regional adaptability than hybrids.

There is concern that in the near future, society could lose its agricultural diversity. To prevent this, American gardeners are learning the ritual that guarantees the survival of unique plants from the past–saving seeds.

Horticulturist Kay Timmis of Olympia, Washington, takes pride in two favorite heirlooms whose seeds she saves. One is the Matucana sweet pea that dates back to 1699. The light-and-dark-purple bloom saturates a room with its scent. The other is a French pumpkin named red etampes. The shell is a burning red-orange, and the large pumpkin's squatty shape reminds Kay of Cinderella's carriage pumpkin.

The "old-fashioned garden" now has double meaning. It is old-fashioned because large segments of our new-fashioned society are no longer gardening; it is old-fashioned in a second sense if the seeds sown in it are heirlooms.

An organization formed to encourage seed-saving is the International Seed Saving Institute. ISSI participates in seed self-reliance projects as far away as Kyrgyzstan (bordering China), Korea, Russia, Haiti, Honduras, and Mexico. Their goal is to help teach one million gardeners how to save garden seeds. ISSI recommends that every gardener save at least their own seeds from the five most popular vegetables: peas, beans, lettuce, tomatoes, and peppers.

The Root of the Matter: Seeds are perishable. Varieties will become extinct without deliberate action to collect and preserve them. What a contrast to the seeds of God's Word! How interesting that Jesus Christ compared the words of God to seed. Though Earth may be threatened by vanishing plant varieties, God's Word will never be lost or forgotten. It is planted in fertile hearts and propagated in yielded lives.

The Fragrance of Praise: I thank You, God, for the invincibility of Your Word.

Garden Tools: Learn about the International Seed Saving Institute (ISSI) at this web site: http://www.seedsave.org

Wildflowers: The moon and stars watermelon is a prime example of an heirloom variety that was presumed lost, was happily rediscovered in rural Missouri, and whose seeds are now regarded as precious.

Watch Where You Step

He who walks with the wise grows wise,
but a companion of fools suffers harm.
PROVERBS 13:20 NIV

Never underestimate the power of influence—it sticks even to the soles of your shoes, as Linda Fuller learned long ago.

The earliest influence upon Linda's life was her parents' love of gardening. She grew up on a farm where her father grew peppermint, alfalfa, wheat, carrot seed, and potatoes, and her mother grew flowers in abundance. Linda's childhood play included the creation of mud pies decorated with pansy petals and ornamental leaves. She remembers helping her mother weed when she was only seven years old. Sounding apologetic, Linda said, "I like to weed."

Her love of sunshine, soil, and plants influenced Linda's choice of summertime employment during her high school years. Hoeing weeds in three-foot-high peppermint fields in the small Oregon town of Madras was a popular wage earner for students. For eight to ten hours a day, she worked and sweated as she and mostly female workers exchanged girl talk while yanking weeds and leaving them to wilt.

During harvest, the mint was cut and laid in rows like hay. Then it was chopped and collected. Thus, in late summer, Linda traded her hoe for the steering wheel of a truck and delivered mint leaves to the distilling chamber. She recalls nightfall when she'd wait in the truck line and gaze through the window at falling stars. "I never realized how many shooting stars there were until I began to stargaze; it's a great memory."

A full day amid acres of peppermint had a permeating influence! The fragrance of mint clung to her shoes and clothing. She carried the fresh scent long after she punched the time clock and left her tangy work site.

The smell of peppermint oil will always be associated with her recollections of family. "When I drive through central Oregon, I know I'm getting close to home when I see the junipers and the Cascade mountain range. Mt. Hood is only fifty miles from our farm. But the welcome perfume of peppermint is like a fragrant gateway. Some daughters remember their father smelling like Old Spice aftershave. My dad smelled like peppermint."

Linda's love of peppermint is obvious in her hobby of gourmet cooking. "I grow three or four kinds of mint and use them in Vietnamese spring rolls and in Thai and Indian dishes." Peppermint at the family farm, on the summer job, and in her ethnically diverse diet has had an enduring influence upon Linda.

The Root of the Matter: Like the redolence of peppermint, influence is invisible but powerful. I have a close-knit group of women with whom I've been friends for many years. We are often together. But long after our luncheons, retreats, or nights out, their influence lingers. The positive effect of their outlook and warmth clings to me from head to toe, from heart to soul. We absorb the bouquet of the people who surround us. Avoid the company of stinkweeds and walk in fields of peppermint.

The Fragrance of Praise: Thank You, God, for the tantalizing aroma of virtuous company.

Garden Tools: The following *Mentha* plants grow well in all geographical zones: golden apple mint *(gentiles),* peppermint *(piperita),* spearmint *(spicata),* and apple mint *(suaveolens).*

Wildflowers: Give someone a potted mint plant with a note attached: "Our acquaintance (friendship, relationship, marriage, etc.) was 'mint' to be."

Never Say, "Just a Seed"

*Now faith is being sure of what we hope for
and certain of what we do not see.*
HEBREWS 11:1 NIV

Another spring, another packet of seeds. Each time I shake a palmful into my hand, I ponder the wonder of a seed. I am awestruck. Compressed inside is a set of detailed instructions. Therein, God keeps safely His designs.

Seeds are marvels of nature. Tiny depositories of mystery. Miniature storehouses entrusted with a plan. They contain proposals that will take form as leaves, flowers, vines, trunks, shrubs, and every other expression of plant life. Though varied in size, every shell is pregnant with a beatific notion of God.

I feel a thrill when I prepare a row for seeds, whether forming a trench with my fingers in a tray of potting soil or dragging my trowel the length of a flower bed. I find the process of planting a seed the most fundamental and sacred act of gardening, for in that moment, I join the Creator of all things green in bringing to life an idea born in His mind.

I settle a few seeds of morning glory in one spot, scatter wild-flowers in a different patch, and fill an S-curved row with snap-dragon hopefuls. Once the seeds are planted, they release the design imprinted within. Days and weeks pass until unveiled is the above-ground creation that was locked inside the diminutive seed. Once a mere dot in my palm is now a cosmos in a vase.

Reflecting on this miracle helps me understand what Jesus meant when He said, "If you have faith as small as a mustard seed, you can say to this mountain, 'Move from here to there' and it will move. Nothing will be impossible for you" (Matthew 17:20).

Could it be that tucked inside all humankind is a blueprint for the impossible, similar to that which resides in a seed? When God settles us in environments that nurture growth, we can accomplish what faithless people say is impossible. We can become all that God intended. Faith is the latent power abiding within, smaller than a mustard seed, but powerful enough to fulfill God's purposes.

Once faith is planted in the human heart, God will do the rest. He'll bring sunshine and rain and even help us pull out the weeds until miracles bloom.

The Root of the Matter: If we want flowers in our garden, we must plant flower seeds. If we want different varieties, we must plant seeds that hold those designs. But if we hope to see answers to prayer, we must sow faith. Never say, "Just a seed." For if it is a seed of faith, it will move mountains.

The Fragrance of Praise: What a revelation, dear God! I am imprinted with Your plan, and faith will give birth to it!

Garden Tools: A stainless steel spade is preferred over one of carbon steel. Though stainless steel costs more, it is rustproof, and soil will fall away from the spade more readily. Alternative tools have nonstick coatings, but the protective film will eventually wear off.

Wildflowers: Herbs mentioned in the Bible are aloe, coriander, dill, frankincense, marjoram, myrrh, sage, and wormwood.

Languages, Spoken and Grown

It is written, "As surely as I live," says the Lord,
"every knee will bow before me;
every tongue will confess to God."
ROMANS 14:11 NIV

During the depression, Marie's family owned no refrigerator and lived on stew that contained ten cents' worth of steak or burger, or one soup bone per week. Yet poverty did not deprive her mother of a new hydrangea each spring. She'd give Marie a quarter to buy just one plant.

The family had left war-threatened Holland, but Marie's father found no steady employment in Canada. Finally, with money from the sale of his life insurance, he bought a confectionary store with a house upstairs. His new income enabled Marie's mother to buy more hydrangeas. Today, Marie grows two in her mother's memory. Though young when both parents died, Marie enjoyed twenty years with God-fearing, garden-loving parents who favorably imprinted her life.

In addition to her parents' influence, Marie learned valuable lessons in Dutch schools. "We were taught religion and domestics," she said. "A nearby garden was one of our tutors."

Though she had to learn two languages when the family moved to Canada, she always graduated at the top of her form. In two years, she became fluent in English and accomplished in grammar. Her grasp for languages was evident again when she excelled in French during high school.

When Marie married, her husband's asthma prompted their move to Washington State. At forty-nine, she followed a dream and enrolled at Eastern Washington College, earning a degree in French. Her mastery won her a position on the college staff; she worked thirteen years in the Modern Language Department. While there, she availed herself of free courses and studied Japanese and Chinese.

Marie speaks English, Dutch, Norwegian, French, Japanese, Chinese, and a bit of "tourist" Russian. The eighth language she failed to mention was the one she spoke while walking me through her gardens—the language of horticulture. Her knowledge and experience with green things is blended with her international appreciation. Like Marie, her large garden speaks foreign languages.

One flowered, pebbled bed seats a Japanese lantern. A tall, rusted, Mexican figure sits atop a raised bed of perennial geraniums. Her Dutch currant bush produces a red berry used in a tasty sauce for farina pudding. Adding a touch of China, Marie shaped her Pfitzer juniper into a bonsai. She pointed out an Irish gunnera plant whose leaf grows six feet wide. A Canadian aunt, who hoped to die "with my boots on," gave her the gooseberry bush she prizes, along with a handcrafted birdhouse for chickadees. Marie has an extraordinary contribution of French art gracing her garden. An espaliered crab apple tree that she has trained for twenty-five years adorns her redwood fence. The trunk is cut even with the top of the fence line, and four branches on each side stretch twelve feet outward, clinging obediently to fence boards. Marie has learned well the language of plants and peoples.

The Root of the Matter: Language is a bridge toward understanding. Though you may speak only your native
tongue, why not encourage international unity with
geographical and ethnic expressions in your garden?
Include plants that are indigenous to other countries.

The Fragrance of Praise: Thank You, God, for the
impartiality of Your love, which unites people of every
language.

Garden Tools: Worm castings (waste) are an international
fertilizer.

Wildflowers: The gardening philosophy of France teaches
man to impose his will upon nature as in the case of
espaliers (plants or trees trained to grow flat against a
support or wall).

If Lonely I'd Known

We have different gifts, according to the grace given us.
ROMANS 12:6 NIV

E ver shuffled through a group of people at a national gathering and found yourself bemused by a conversation you overhear? Two people are talking flowers and trees. Though both speak English, their exchanges include a bit of Latin–*Chamaecyparis speciosa,* and a word that sounds like French–"I'd love to create a *parterre,* but I've run out of room." Next, one asks a strange question, "What's your zone?" You wonder, *Are they getting personal?*

If you're a nongardener, you'd likely move across the room and drum up conversation with someone besides the curious pair discussing the zany, or rather, zone-y topic.

However, their conversation was neither bizarre nor personal, nor was the subject matter cryptic. You were in the company of devoted gardeners. The answer to the question, "What's your zone?" is the most telling information one gardener can share with another.

A look at the U.S. Department of Agriculture's map of North America shows eleven plant hardiness zones based on winter minimum temperatures. For more specific climate zones, consult the *Sunset* garden book maps, which define even more climate zones within each of the five major regions just in the United States: Northeast; Southeast; Midwest, High Plains, and Western Mountains; Southwest; and Pacific Northwest. The *Sunset* scheme considers not just winter minimums, but also figures in summer highs, length of growing season, humidity, and rainfall patterns to give a more accurate picture of what will grow where. To illustrate: If you live in Atascadero, California, your North American hardiness zone is nine, while your *Sunset* climate zone is seven.

The zone in which you live is the most important factor in determining what will grow in your garden. Boulevards in cities of the Pacific Northwest are not lined with palm trees for obvious reasons. Tropical varieties do not favor cold temperatures. While citrus trees thrive in the Southeast, apple trees favor the higher altitudes of the

Northwest. Many annuals that bloom year-round in the Southwest will freeze in the Northeast and Northwest. Climate, soil, and latitude can be friend or foe.

When I learn to maximize the possibilities in my geographical zone and resign to its limitations, I am God's wise apprentice. In the same way, finding the most beneficial environment for my abilities makes me a more effective person, not to mention a happier one.

The Root of the Matter: Involve yourself in activities that suit your assets, aptitudes, and God-granted gifts. Don't volunteer outside your zone. Ask me to write a brochure, give a speech, or decorate a room. But please, don't ask me to help at a hospital or to prepare a meal for fifty. Learn where you grow best so you don't wilt while performing a service that doesn't match your talents. If you're a water lily, you won't last long in the Sahara!

The Fragrance of Praise: Thank You, wise God, for my

special requirements. They adapt me for a custom contribution in the seed rows of life.

Garden Tools: "Zone in" at your local library. General gardening is Dewey decimal number 635. Spend an hour scanning titles on bookshelves and check out an armful of texts. Record noteworthy information in a garden journal.

Wildflowers: "He who plants a seed beneath the sod, and waits to see, believes in God."   AUTHOR UNKNOWN

Rarely a Hole-in-One

In his heart, a man plans his course,
but the LORD determines his steps.
PROVERBS 16:9 NIV

Though Tim Ansett superintends the grounds at Manito Golf and Country Club, quite often God superimposes His plans over Tim's. How does that make a responsible guy feel? Matter-of-factly, Tim answered, "A sovereign God is in charge, so flex with the changes."

But Tim doesn't putt around. Tending grass slopes involves far more than riding a commercial-size mower and controlling dandelions.

Tim took an interest in golf after high school and soon learned a person could enjoy a life on the course not only by packing a bag of clubs. To qualify himself as superintendent, he earned a B.S. in crop and soil sciences and an M.S. in horticulture. His specialty is turf-grass management.

In 1922 the eighteen-hole course opened. The PGA championship tournament was hosted there twenty-two years later. The original buildings have been remodeled and expanded to include a large clubhouse, a pro shop, a swimming pool, and a dining room that seats the private club's four hundred members.

"Do you ever get to golf?" I asked. Silly question. That's like asking the vegetable gardener if he ever snacks on the first ripe tomato or hoses off a freshly dug carrot and eats it on the spot. Tim said, "Theoretically, a superintendent should play golf at least weekly to inspect the course from the viewpoint of the golfer. It's part of my job." But sometimes his maintenance duties prevail over theory and squeeze out the game.

Tim speaks from twenty-four seasons of experience. "The unexpected constantly alters my agenda. It snows in May. Equipment breaks down. Short supplies delay projects. Staff fail to report. The golf schedule changes. In 1989, one hundred trees toppled in a windstorm." Problems result in a lot of long days that score over par.

"Long ago I was struck by a Bible proverb that says, 'A man's heart plans his way, but the LORD directs his steps' (Proverbs 16:9 NKJV). I'm getting better at remembering that fact when I'm forced to revise my daily list," he said.

Tim's commendable attitude isn't consistent, he confesses. He gets teed off at times. "My first reaction to interruptions and problems is often pretty human. But I'm learning. My secondary reaction is to accept God's sovereignty in matters like weather changes" and other surprises that slow his career game of maintaining 120 acres.

On some days he even makes a birdie! He accomplishes better than his average. "But I know I've really got it right if I can step back and believe God's still in control when my own plans are canceled."

The Root of the Matter: The fairways of life are similar to those at Manito. Daily, the unexpected strikes everyone, not just groundskeepers. Make your plans, but don't grip them as you would a long iron over a water hazard. God is directing your life even when circumstances interfere with your timetable. Spare yourself frustration with a note at the top of your schedule. "God is in control, always!"

The Fragrance of Praise: Dear God, I praise You for Your greatness; deliver me from a miniature concept of my big God.

Garden Tools: An easy way to remember when to fertilize your lawn is to schedule your treatments near these four holidays: Easter, Memorial Day, Independence Day, and Veteran's Day.

Wildflowers: "The safest way to remain in control is to surrender the controls to God."   ANONYMOUS

$\mathcal{PURR}$-ennial Garden

When a man's ways please the LORD,
He makes even his enemies to be at peace with him.
PROVERBS 16:7 NKJV

A black kitten is credited for launching the Meyer Cat Garden. When Chris Sheppard brought home orphaned Oliver, she determined her rescued stray would never roam outdoors. The cat "with the soul of a poet," said Chris, "inspired the need for gardens."

Oliver joined the Meyer family, composed of mother Mary, father Del, sisters Della, ViAnn, and third sister Chris, and her husband Mark.

To offer their cats the luxury of nature, plus protection from predators, Chris thought, *Why not build an outdoor run?* Del completed a ten-by-thirty-foot enclosure with lawn, ledges, potted catmint and catnip, and feline favorites–the ornamental grasses of eulalia, sedge, and quaking. But the Meyers also provided birdsong and a garden view outside the enclosure for their growing family of eight felines.

As the garden expanded, Del constructed 180 feet of boardwalk, which leads visitors on a tour through the acre of groomed vegetation. The garden entryway is topped with a handcrafted comic cat. Signs decorated with cats and metal-art cat depictions reinforce the feline theme. Cat statues and other garden ornaments establish mini themes for various sections of the garden, such as the children-and-cats sector, and the big-cats alley. Other thematic beds include an eighty-foot perennial display, a shade bed of hosta, lamium, and astilbe, and a bed of oriental specimens like the tri-color Japanese maple. A cat topiary, a squirrel-feeding station, brightly painted birdhouses and feeders, dazzling gazing balls, a resting bench, and a pergola are added attractions. A wood-carved cat stands guard on each side of a bridge, which spans a double pond. Circulating water tumbles down a waterfall. An arched trellis is covered with white clematis, and nearby, a resin Cheshire cat hangs from a tree branch. It is truly a wonderland garden.

Everyone (but Mother) works the gardens. Chris weeds, Della waters, and ViAnn specializes in container plants. Del, a retired carpenter, is always building or repairing. Mark, who built many of the raised beds, incorporated his love of trains in a prize creation—a waist-high bed containing an electric train. Tiny pointed shrubs double as tall trees admired by imaginary passengers. The train chugs past a lake and through a tunnel grown over by woolly thyme.

One more family member, a toy spaniel, deserves mention. Ziggy, the six-pound French Papillon, was selected based on the breed's reputation as the most catlike among dogs. Cabbage roses fill Ziggy's honorary garden beds.

The Meyer Garden is a certified Washington State Backyard Wildlife Sanctuary. With planning, effort, and a few controls, domestic cats and wildlife can coexist peacefully in a garden milieu. Chickadees, nuthatches, swallows, sparrows, grosbeaks, and red and gold finches sing and nest near the cat enclosure. It's win-win for the cats, plant life, wildlife, and one wee dog—natural enemies appreciating the company of one another.

The Root of the Matter: Do you suppose that with some extra effort and self-control, we, too, could abide peaceably with our adversaries? We may not agree, but we can strive to dwell together amiably. Loving our enemies lessens hostility and may even win us a friend.

The Fragrance of Praise: Dearest God, thank You for wisdom to live compatibly in a world of tensions.

Garden Tools: Make gardening a family affair. Divisions of responsibility allow each person to labor in an area of choice.

Wildflowers: A recent Gallup poll reports that 42 percent of all American households have gardens. Flower gardeners spend an average of $102 each year on their hobby, and vegetable gardeners spend $84.

Garden Compensation

"Come to me, all you who are weary and burdened,
and I will give you rest.
For my yoke is easy and my burden is light."
MATTHEW 11:28, 30 NIV

It makes life a lot easier, if you're doing something you like," said Jerry Keevy. The compensating joy of gardening eased the less appealing demands of life for Jerry; his father, Charles; and his grandfather, Franklin.

"In 1878, my granddad homesteaded far from the nearest town," said Jerry. "Before his first garden produced, he walked forty-five miles to buy food. He broke ground with crude tools and scattered wheat seed from a burlap sack. Next he planted a garden." He loved both gardening and farming, but his son, Charles, cared only for gardening. "My father never grew fond of farming," said Jerry.

When Jerry's grandmother died suddenly, Charles, the eldest son, was obliged to remain on the farm to help his father support his younger sister and three brothers. His hours in the field were drudgery, but fall bulb planting and springtime blooms were his compensation. Years later, he sold the farm and moved to town where he planted a rose garden.

Like his father, Charles, Jerry was not fond of farming but enjoyed gardening. "I was never more than a step behind my grand-dad throughout my childhood. I helped him plant squash, cabbage, melons, tomatoes, raspberries, onions, carrots, beans, peas, potatoes, cucumbers, and lettuce. We also planted apple and cherry trees that gave memorable yields."

When Jerry married, his wife Marie said she never got a chance to garden. "Jerry's mother assigned me to the kitchen." Marie was content; she'd rather be indoors than outdoors. But her mother-in-law was passionate about gardening. One year she harvested enough fruits and vegetables to can fifteen hundred quarts.

Upon retirement, Jerry and Marie moved to Lilac Plaza, a senior community. The fourteen-story complex is surrounded by well-groomed lawns and a centerpiece rose garden of hybrid teas and floribundas. Residents have traditionally been hired to nurture the 128 rosebushes. Among the two hundred retirees, there's always a gardener eager to volunteer. Jerry was first in line when the last rosarian gave up the job. "Jerry has to be outside," Marie commented. He learned much about roses from his father. "His dad had over one hundred bushes," Marie recalled. "For every occasion, people gave him a rosebush; nothing made him happier."

Now, when Jerry works the rose bed, residents often call to him, "You're working too hard!" But he just smiles. He's there by choice, to weed, spade, mulch, prune, or deadhead spent blossoms.

The downside of supervising the rose garden is enforcing the rule, "Don't pick the flowers!" But there are exceptions. Some of the bushes memorialize past residents. Spouses who donated them sometimes cut blooms from those bushes. And Jerry is allowed to pick bouquets for some of the Plaza events.

From 1878, when Jerry's grandfather began homesteading, to year 2000 at Lilac Plaza, are 122 years of happy gardening for three generations. Like the Keevys, everyone needs a pleasurable outlet. For thousands, it is gardening. How true it is—"Life's a lot easier if you're doing something you like."

The Root of the Matter: Many people are needlessly fearful of God's will. They suppose that obeying Him will mean surrendering activities they love. On the contrary, God is not stingy with the gift of joy. He is delighted when we experience satisfaction in gratifying pastimes. Happy diversions refresh us, and often they draw us closer to God.

The Fragrance of Praise: Dear God, thank You for Your presence in the midst of all the pursuits of life.

Garden Tools: Feed roses with a granular slow-release fertilizer designed for them. Or, apply well-rotted manure or a dousing of fish emulsion.

Wildflowers: Jerry started school at age five and took his naps on the teacher's lap. In seven years, he never missed a day. The only time he was late was the morning he stopped to pick flowers for his teacher.

Urban Garden Solves a Farming Problem

"I am the LORD your God, who teaches you to profit,
Who leads you by the way you should go."
ISAIAH 48:17 NKJV

After visiting with the co-owner of an urban greenhouse garden, I knew I'd met a facilitator. Doug Welch and partner are practicing a solution for the problem plaguing American farmers—the suffocating competition from foreign produce suppliers stocking our supermarkets.

I was welcomed to Okanogan Farms, just twenty-five blocks

south of Spokane, Washington, by a wave from the noticeably tall Welshman. He assured me he's not as tall as the weeds he pulled when he leased the greenhouse a year ago and moved to Spokane from the rural Okanogan Valley. Doug's urban business is named after the rural agricultural region where his partner still lives and tends orchards.

I followed Doug inside to tour half of the seventy-thousand-square-foot structures. Two humming, fifty-million BTU boilers regulate the greenhouse temperature. The operation grows perennials, annuals, and herbs, and offers some produce delivered from rural farms.

To minimize government regulation and encourage the health of employees and clients, Doug chose the organic method of gardening. Thus, his helpers include nematodes, ladybugs (four hundred thousand!), and predatory wasps, which patrol the plants. "We also do a lot of pest pinching," he added. "Organic gardening is labor-intensive, but we can afford extra employees because we aren't laden with transportation costs. Our customers come to us." One hundred happy members, who collect a share of produce each week, support the operation.

After a stroll past rows of vegetables—over forty varieties—I was impressed more by the stature of Doug's vision than the height of the sunlit windows above me.

For years, Doug had watched his farming community's high school graduates leave the Okanogan Valley and pursue careers with a future better than farming. Though Doug and his father come from generations of farmers, they faced a similar fate. Insufficient revenue from farming alone allowed them to farm only part-time. But after years as a computer programmer, Doug still hankered to be a full-time farmer. He believes the urban greenhouse is an economic answer for the rural farmer.

Community Supported Agriculture (CSA), the concept on which Okanogan Farms was established, is one solution for the problem posed by lower-priced foreign providers who are driving farmers out of business. Large greenhouse gardens like Okanogan, located near large cities, provide rural farms a nearby outlet for their crops, saving farmers the exorbitant costs of shipping to distant markets. As rural and urban farms work together in this way, they can compete with foreign providers. "And the beauty of it," said Doug, "is that populations in Spokane and vicinity could support hundreds more urban farms like my own."

Though he still accepts contracts for computer programming, the sixty-year-old businessman cherishes the farm lifestyle. "Farming isn't for everyone, but it should be a choice for people who love it; CSA is one option."

Solutions are futile without a facilitator to pioneer new concepts. Doug set that example by fathering a business and birthing his vision. An entrepreneur in overalls, he would make proud the grandmother who told him, "You were born to hold a shovel in your hands."

The Root of the Matter: Each of us was born to herald a message or promote a concept. What vision is God waiting for you to facilitate?

The Fragrance of Praise: Thank You, God, that You are the Source of every solution.

Garden Tools: Doug contends that one of the best sources for information on gardening is NASA.

Wildflowers: "Some people calm their stress with a candy bar; I head off mine with a spading fork."

A SLENDER ANONYMOUS GARDENER

Garden Restoration

Restore to me the joy of your salvation.
PSALM 51:12 NIV

Like historic landmarks, designed landscapes are now eligible as historic sites for local, state, and national registers. One such landscape was recently nominated for the Spokane Register of Historic Places. Preservationists are seeking grants and donations to restore the garden that once adorned the property of two prominent families in Spokane, Washington. The garden chronicles a vision, its fulfillment, later ruin, and the proposed restoration.

The garden of the Moore-Turner estate was once "the pride of aristocratic and fashionable Seventh Avenue." People boarded trolleys in the early 1900s to view a row of mansions owned by the elite, particularly, the Tudor Revival style home of F. Rockwood Moore with its hillside terraces.

In 1884, Moore stood on Fourth Avenue and admired a two-thousand-foot elevation of hillside with massive rock outcroppings and visualized terraces on the sloping five acres. After buying the property, he hired famed architect, Kirtland Cutter, to design his three-story home. By 1888, the rock-faced terraces he envisioned were also completed.

In 1895, Moore died at age forty-three. George Turner, a lawyer, territorial judge, U.S. senator, and mining investor, purchased the property a year later. He commissioned major remodeling from 1911–1913 with the supervision of landscape designer, Hugh Bryan. The Olmsted brothers, landscape architects for New York City's Central Park, influenced the Arts and Crafts garden style suggested by Bryan. For seventeen years, the Turners embellished the property with stonework, manicured lawns, hedges, and plant specimens imported from Holland, England, France, and the Orient. Archival pictures show blooming spiraea draping the lawn, iris encircling the pond, and rosebushes lining a pathway.

The terraced garden included a pergola with carved beams and basalt piers, a seventy-foot trout-stocked pond with aquatic plants and waterfall, a stone house for growing mushrooms, a reflecting pool, a rose arbor, a teahouse, a conservatory, rock stairways, and crushed gravel paths wending throughout.

Judge Turner and Bertha, a childless couple, traveled worldwide and entertained lavishly. Bertha, previously an Alabama debutante, hosted weddings, garden soirees, elaborate receptions, garden clubs, and sundry parties. If the still-standing horse chestnut, linden, or elm trees could talk, they would tell of visits from dignitaries like Theodore Roosevelt.

Turner died at eighty-one in 1932. Before Bertha's death seven years later, she lost her home of thirty-six years in a mortgage default during the Great Depression. Liquidators found no buyer for the magnificent estate. To the despair and astonishment of citizens, the house was demolished in 1940 to avoid payment of property taxes.

Presently, the ruins of the Moore-Turner garden are Pioneer Park. With the help of an endowment, the city park board bought the property in 1945. For the next fifty-five years, the glorious garden, once described by a real estate developer as "unsurpassed in American home grounds," surrendered to the domination of native vegetation. In time, overgrowth disguised stone stairways, pathways, and pools. Today, wild honeysuckle, syringa, Oregon grape, and brush have overtaken the select varieties planted by the Turners. Harsh winters have also deteriorated property structures. What remains are crumbled, though identifiable, remnants of the past.

However, Spokane preservationists are optimistic about the restoration. A master plan is underway. Bertha Turner's scrapbooks, which document details of the original garden, will greatly benefit replication of the famous turn-of-the-century garden.

The Root of the Matter: The vision, fulfillment, ruin, and restoration of the Moore-Turner garden remind us of a similar sequence of events. As a Father, God envisioned His children fellowshipping with Him in unbroken harmony. In the Garden of Eden, His intention was fulfilled only temporarily. Disobedience brought ruin. Two thousand years later, Jesus Christ restored the relationship between God and humankind by taking the penalty for our sins. It's a story more poignant than any garden account ever told. Best of all, there's a surprise ending; for those who receive Jesus as Savior, the Garden of Eden still exists.

The Fragrance of Praise: Thank You, God, for restoring ruined lives.

Garden Tools: The web site for the National Register of Historic Places is http://www.cr.nps.gov/nr/index.htm

Wildflowers: Heritage gardens are popular in England and Canada and are beginning to attract interest in the United States. Visit one nearby.

Morning Muse

"Flowers appear on the earth;
the season of singing has come,
the cooing of doves is heard in our land.
The fig tree forms its early fruit;
the blossoming vines spread their fragrance.
Arise, come, my darling;
my beautiful one, come with me."
SONG OF SONGS 2:12–13 NIV

One summer at daybreak, I was overcome with the joy of my garden and the rewards of being a gardener. I felt jubilant in every molecule of my body. Filled with thanksgiving, my heart sang.

"I'm grateful for the multibloom mélange of color filling the view through my dining room window, a picture more perfect than a framed original by a classical artist.

"I'm grateful, God, for sunshine relaxing my bowed back when I kneel beside flower beds and for dulcimer-like birdsong that accompanies my labors.

"I'm grateful for the peculiar satisfaction of pulling weeds from damp soil, for grit under my fingernails, and grateful, too, that soil washes off!

"I'm grateful for the pleasant chore of planting palm-size root balls of petunias, pansies, and marigolds and that a task as simple as lifting a trowelful of soil makes a home for a youthful plant.

"I'm grateful for the science of growth, the palette of flower and leaf colors, and the varieties of form found only in a garden.

"I'm grateful for the cycle of seasons, succeeding always and returning each year to honor me with a harvest more mature than the previous.

"I'm grateful for the quiet company of helper insects.

"I'm grateful for the unceasing opportunity to learn new lessons, to plant different species, and to try new garden experiments.

"I'm grateful for the knowledge I've gained because my garden insists I understand what it needs to be healthy and productive.

"I'm grateful for bouquets to share, greenery to gather, and pinecones to collect.

"I'm grateful for garden contrasts—red maple leaves and white dusty miller, dainty sweet woodruff and showy rhododendrons, furry lamb's ear and prickly pine needles.

"I'm grateful for sunshine that resurrects winter sleepers and for frost that announces the end of summer.

"I'm grateful for serene interludes when I rest and thrill to the view of God's handiwork assisted by my stewardship.

"I'm grateful for the gift of gardens and to the Creator Who fashioned their foliage and flowers and fragrance, their trees, shrubs, and vines, their vegetables and fruits that I and others are privileged to tend.

The Root of the Matter: The garden boasts of God's handiwork. Look closely at a leaf as it glistens in the morning sun, or count the ways insects make cocoons on the leaves and stems of a tree. Inhale the fragrance of wild honeysuckle or jasmine, and give praise to the One Who created such pleasure.

The Fragrance of Praise: God of deepest root and highest treetop, I praise You for Your wondrous creation; my heart swells with thankfulness.

Garden Tools: Advice for indoor gardeners: (1) When cutting off the brown tips of leaves on potted plants, leave a narrow brown border. Cutting into live tissue will cause further drying and dieback. (2) Don't use leaf shine products; they may clog leaf pores. Instead, enhance leaf luster by wiping them with a damp sponge.

Wildflowers: "Mistress Mary, quite contrary, how does your garden grow? Silver bells, and cockleshells, and pretty maids all in a row." Not merely a garden poem, this Mother Goose rhyme was a political satire describing Mary, Queen of Scots (d. 1587). The "silver bells," her jewelry; the "cockleshells," her epicurean palate; and the "pretty maids," her four royal maids of honor.

A Sunflower of a Gardener

' "Man does not live on bread alone,
but on every word that comes from the mouth of God.' "
MATTHEW 4:4 NIV

I'm acquainted with no other gardener who beats April to the draw and drives 325 miles to a warmer climate to see daffodils in bloom. The day I interviewed Nancy Harbert, her living room was alive with bouquets of the cheery yellow trumpeters she had transported home.

In childhood, Nancy's innate gardening interests became apparent. The neighbors seldom mowed their lawn, and she could not abide their neglect. It was not her father or brother who volunteered, but it was Nancy, then a grade-schooler, who hauled out the mower and buzzed over the neighbor's waist-high grass. Later, she overheard the neighbor couple arguing over which of them had mowed the lawn!

Nancy's family home was small with little yard, but there she experimented with sprouting seeds indoors and grew hollyhocks alongside the house.

Like other citizens who planted victory gardens during World War II, Nancy and her father harvested lettuce, peas, beans, potatoes, and other staples, products of their patriotism. The only years Nancy was not dabbling in the dirt was a stint during high school when the family lived in a residential community that hired a gardener who relieved--or deprived--everyone of gardening.

The past thirty-eight years, she and her husband have toiled in their large garden of scalloped beds filled with bulbs, annuals, and mature perennials, vines, and shrubs. Nancy is sensitive to the microclimates in her yard. "I've hit on the truth of what works here and pretty much stick to what's proven successful."

One summer day after touring Nancy's garden, I followed her through a gate and behind her fence to the alley. I happened to know that particular alley was a depository for debris--pine needles, leaves, and other dead growth. But on the narrow strip between Nancy's fence and the alleyway stood a pristine row of hollyhocks growing in tidy weed-free beds. I was impressed!

Eventide in Nancy's garden has opened a new perspective. She and Bill are hobby astronomers. They spend evenings viewing the heavens through their eight-inch telescope. Nancy has noticed that white blooms like those of alyssum and her large yellow and orange marigolds are particularly reflective under starlight. With feet planted in her glorious garden and eyes gazing upward, she is enveloped with breathtaking beauty.

Looking into Nancy's face is like looking upon a sunflower. She wears a perennial smile set in a round face framed in blonde hair. Her garden is her therapy even while she wrestles a chronic physical ailment. It's her place to relax. "I settle in a lawn chair and think, 'This is truly beautiful.' "

A quote stamped on a T-shirt she purchased at the Skagit Valley Tulip Festival best communicates her sentiments. "If I had but two loaves of bread, I would sell one and buy flowers, for they would feed my soul."

The Root of the Matter: Like gardening, many good hobbies can be therapeutic. But man cannot live on bread, flowers, or hobbies alone. The Bible says that only God's Word will sustain us. Flowers point us to Jesus Christ, the "Lily of the Valley" and the "Rose of Sharon." Only He can satisfy the soul.

The Fragrance of Praise: Thank You, God, for the likeness of Christ in the petals of a flower.

Garden Tools: Though some gardeners think white blooms are a stark contributor to the garden, they are magnificent additions amidst brilliant color.

Wildflowers: In 1859, the Reverend Henry Ward Beecher purported that a love of flowers would "beget early rising, industry, habits of close observation, and of reading. . .and unfold in the heart an enlarged, unstraightened, ardent piety."

Vital Attraction

But the fruit of the Spirit is
love, joy, peace, patience, kindness, goodness,
faithfulness, gentleness and self-control.
GALATIANS 5:22–23 NIV

Looking especially nice today? Longing for a compliment? I'm keenly aware the words "beautiful" or "gorgeous" are unlikely to be part of behind-my-back discussions. But, hey, most of us are just as delighted when someone says, "You're attractive!" It means there is something about us that draws others—something that attracts. Usually something illusive, rather than one's face or figure. Could it be our personality, a sweetness about our nature? Perhaps it's charm or kindness.

Among the goals we might set for our gardens is that they be attractive. Unless they are attractive in the literal sense, we will never invite the visitation of those lovely winged flowers that flutter and hover amidst flora while seeking nectar. I'm speaking of butterflies and hummingbirds.

Ornaments of the garden, both living and inanimate, are all part of the ambiance. These range from hummingbirds and butterflies to redwood benches and animal statuaries. Benches can be built and statues can be purchased, but "winged flowers" must be courted.

Bushes that excrete sugar invite these flighty guests to our gardens. Both butterflies and hummingbirds feed on nectar. Plant hollyhock, yarrow, sunflower, dill, sage, flossflower, candytuft, aster, phlox, or *buddleia,* commonly called butterfly bush, if you want butterflies to frequent your yard. Tiger swallowtails, cabbage whites, sulfurs, and other butterflies will imbibe nectar from these natural sweet factories. Cosmos, milkweed, ageratum, annual orange safflower, heliotrope, and sweet alyssum also summon butterflies.

Hummingbirds prefer tubular-shaped flowers and are attracted to color, not smell. Red is their favorite hue. They will investigate even a red shirt draped across a lawn chair. Orange and pink also draw them. But commercially prepared hummingbird mixes are usually red. Chinese wisteria, red azaleas, fuchsia, impatiens, catmint, red petunias, salvia, and annual nasturtium are plants that entreat the presence of hummingbirds.

Not everyone is a beauty queen. But anyone can be attractive. How? By offering the sweet spirit of understanding, compassion, and helpfulness. I can't afford a surgeon capable of changing the contour of my nose, but I can make myself attractive by developing the graces of winsome character.

If I were to become a plant, I'd choose to be a variety that is nectar-rich and scarlet red. Such plants invite the companionship of both birds and butterflies in the same way that a sweet nature wins the companionship of many friends.

The Root of the Matter: Beauty attracts people, but character wins their favor. Esther, whose story is recorded in the Old Testament, went through twelve months of beauty treatments before she was presented as a candidate for marriage to the king. Though he chose Esther because of her physical beauty, it was her character that later influenced him to spare her nation from genocide. Beautiful character—that's what we need!

The Fragrance of Praise: What a challenge to remember that goodness attracts like a magnet!

Garden Tools: Avoid all pesticides and poisons if you plan to attract butterflies and hummingbirds. Use organic pest controls or antibacterial soaps to control noxious pests, or introduce insects like ladybugs or lacewings for natural control. Protect the broods of birds from the claws of cats by planting a climbing rose on the sunny side of the tree.

Wildflowers: Hummingbirds are the smallest species of birds. Their wings flap and twist, moving from twenty-two to seventy-eight times per second, producing the hum that gives them their name. They are the only birds capable of flying backward.

I Love to Weed!

See to it that no one misses the grace of God
and that no bitter root grows up to cause trouble and defile many.
HEBREWS 12:15 NIV

Last spring, I let a large bed flourish with weeds. The beguiling starts had me fooled. When the young shoots emerged, they looked innocent. They bore no resemblance to weeds I recognized readily and yanked without hesitation. *Has some good seed blown in from a neighbor's yard? Something delightful, perhaps?* I wondered.

Rather than take the time to identify the invasive shoots in question, I let them grow, until at last I determined they were weeds. Fortunately, it was not too late to eradicate them. The roots were shallow, so it was easy and fun to extricate them by handfuls. But I had transgressed the cardinal rule of weed control—prevention.

That experience last spring was a flashback to my gardening fear of earlier years. As a beginner, I was afraid to weed. Not yet familiar with the foliage of either weeds or even desirable plants, I couldn't tell the difference. Sometimes I ignored my doubt and dug up shoots in hopes they were, indeed, weeds. With more experience, I developed an eye for trespassers like clover, shepherd's purse, chickweed, and other common weeds. Now weeds no longer intimidate me. I know "who" they are and I am aggressive when they begin to peek through my soil.

Weeds are unsightly, but worse yet, they are thugs. They rob the soil of water and nutrients intended for cultivated plants. They sometimes harbor diseases and serve as host for pests. Their presence may cause unwanted shade, block adequate air circulation, or crowd crops.

Weeds are no longer a major threat to my garden. My husband applies a pre-emergent in the spring that greatly reduces weed growth. I pull whatever weeds spring up later as soon as I notice them. There's something satisfying about cleaning up the beds— collecting fallen pine needles and tiny branches, dead leaves or expired blossoms. And pulling weeds. I can honestly say, I love to weed.

It's risky business to allow the growth of a mystery plant. If you can't find a picture or description of a weed suspect in a garden book, or if you've moved to a location where you aren't familiar with undesirable growth, cut a sample and take it to a nursery where someone can help you identify it.

Weeds are a lot like peccadilloes of the heart. An offense can cause a bitter spirit. If we let a bad attitude germinate, it will spread, color our personality, affect our behavior, and choke our relationship with God. Removal is the best way to avoid trouble imposed by weeds. It's also the best method for dealing with bitter roots that can overrun the heart. Scripture warns us—bitterness will "cause trouble and defile many."

The Root of the Matter: Weeds rooted in the heart are perhaps more destructive than weeds in the earth. Ill will can quickly invade the spirit and strangle good virtues. We should frequently check our attitudes, watching for upstarts of jealousy, self-pity, or unjustified anger. The slightest temptation should be "nipped in the bud."

The Fragrance of Praise: Thank You, Lord, for Your patience with my reluctance to weed my heart of harmful attitudes.

Garden Tools: Ten common weeds are bindweed, Bermuda grass, crabgrass, curly dock, dandelion, lamb's-quarters, *Oxalis,* redroot, pigweed, and purslane.

Wildflowers: In 1912, C. Austin Miles was studying the story of Mary coming to the Garden of the Sepulcher to visit Jesus' tomb and was inspired to write the famous verses and chorus of the hymn, "In the Garden." According to some polls, it is the second most popular gospel song.

The Garden Venue

"Consider how the lilies grow. They do not labor or spin.
Yet I tell you, not even Solomon in all his splendor
was dressed like one of these."
LUKE 12:27 NIV

A teary-eyed father and a radiant daughter strolled arm in arm beside bushes of laurel and near aroma of lavender. At the sound of a trumpet, they exchanged smiling glances, then walked in synchronized step down a verdant aisle strewn with red and white rose petals. A garden wedding had begun.

In the presence of beaming relatives and sixty guests, Father handed Daughter to her groom. The couple joined hands and faced a kind and mustached judge who stood under a wicker arch festooned with lacy greens and rosebuds. Two pine trees flanked the arch and afforded umbrage from midafternoon sun. In sincere and hushed tones, affirmations of love and vows of commitment were spoken on that warm August day.

"I do," whispered a glowing bride.

"I do," promised a handsome groom.

Among innumerable events transpiring in my garden, my daughter's wedding was the most enchanting. Flowers were the primary decor complementing the most brilliant blossom of all, the bride herself.

Our cedar fence encloses a backyard of scalloped beds containing hostas, daisies, ferns, butterfly bush, coreopsis, lamium, hydrangeas, roses, daylilies, coral bells, astilbes, trumpet vine, flowering quince, *Saxifraga,* hollyhocks, *Rudbeckia, Gaillardia,* and numerous other resplendent residents.

The wedding party and family groups posed for professional pictures before backgrounds of shrubbery and orange daylilies. Hanging baskets of petunias, fuchsia, and Bolivian Jew swung near a poster board of snapshots that traced the couples' childhoods. Roses floated in globes of water on luncheon tables, and mixed bouquets graced counters spread with fine food. A nosegay of daisies and pink roses topped the wedding cake. Boutonnieres decorated lapels of gentlemen in the party, and corsages formalized the attire of ladies. Crowning the bride's head were miniature red rosebuds tucked along a French twist of blonde curls.

A garden is an exquisite site for a wedding. No number of balloons or crepe paper streamers can compete with the celebratory song of flowers and foliage in their natural habitat.

In addition to its esthetics, a garden ought to be useful. When weather permits, always consider your garden as a meeting place. Sometimes we bemoan our small homes and forget we have large yards with nature's unrivaled ornamentation. Give your garden occasion to caress the senses of your visitors with fragrance, color, and variety. My garden also has been host to luncheons, teas, barbecues, sunbathers, prayer groups, and retreaters.

Offer your garden frequently as a venue for gatherings. A host extraordinaire, it needs neither tuxedo nor apron. Garbed in unparalleled natural costume, a garden is a gracious and stunning entertainer.

The Root of the Matter: Hospitality is high on God's list of virtues. He wants us to host gatherings so we might "spur one another on toward love and good deeds" (Hebrews 10:24 NIV). The sanctuary of a garden is a breathtaking place to congregate. Is there some event you could host in your garden?

The Fragrance of Praise: I praise You, God, for the extravagant decor of nature.

Garden Tools: For your garden event, add color by placing pots filled with all-season bloomers among your planted perennials that have finished their cycle of blooming. If guest seating is necessary, check rental companies. Chairs cost around $1.25 each, a small amount when you realize you would otherwise spend far more for indoor decorations.

Wildflowers: The first wedding was conducted in the Garden of Eden.

Dirty Work

"A farmer went out to sow his seed. . . .
some fell along the path and the birds came and ate it up. . .
Still other seed fell on good soil, where it produced a crop—
a hundred, sixty or thirty times what was sown."
MATTHEW 13:3–4, 8 NIV

Gardening begins at the ground level. Soil, a dignified title for dirt, is the necessary environment for seeds, bulbs, and roots that birth or support most plant life. This fact spells dirty work for the gardener.

"Don't make gardening sound so earthy!" you might complain. "Gardening is a science and an art."

True, but much of science occurs below the ground, and rising from the grit and grime is the botanical art that pleases our eyes. If you recoil at the thought of dirty fingernails, perhaps you should change your hobby to coin collecting. Prefer gardening? Then let's get down to earth.

Is your soil sandy, clay, or loam? Soil is made up mostly of three kinds of mineral particles: sand, silt, and clay. The proportion of these particles categorizes the texture of soil. Loam, comprised of roughly equal amounts of all three, is the best combination. Sand allows for drainage and air movement, and clay helps retain moisture and nutrients. Silt particles are smaller than sand and larger than clay.

What does this mean for you as a caretaker? Keep in mind the three things that soil must contribute—moisture, oxygen, and nutrients. Water and nutrients pass quickly through sand, requiring more frequent watering and fertilizing. Because heavy clay soils pack tightly (they stick to your shoes and tools), they retain water and tend to be fertile, though they may remain too soggy for some roots. Loam is about forty percent sand, forty percent silt, and twenty percent clay.

Test your soil texture by putting one inch of dry loose soil in a tall quart jar. Fill the jar with two-thirds water and one teaspoon liquid dish detergent or table salt. Shake the jar thoroughly and let the contents settle for seven days. Then measure the depths of the different layers. You will see the approximate percentages of sand, silt, and clay. (Loam will be three-quarters inch each of sand and silt, and clay will measure less than one-half inch). If this is inconclusive, purchase a soil-testing kit at your local nursery. Or, consult your county extension agent.

What did I learn from God while studying soil samples? Even the dirt tutors us wisely. A balance of sand, silt, and clay makes a blend of premium soil. All my life, balance has proven a dependable guide. Why should I be surprised that balance is a factor in ideal soil?

The Root of the Matter: The more balanced our lives, the
  fewer problems we create. For example, if we work
  too much, we become stressed and dull. If we play too
  much, we fall behind and get frustrated. When we
  blend work and play, along with other essential needs,
  what's the result? A balanced lifestyle, like good soil–
  capable of growing, supporting, and maturing the life

that God planted within us.

The Fragrance of Praise: Thank You, Father, for facts of
nature that reinforce principles of living.

Garden Tools: Partially decomposed leaves make "leaf
mold," which can be turned into the soil and serve as
an organic soil amendment.

Wildflowers: Those who use the expression "dirt cheap"
forget that the gardener's dirt is nutrient rich!

Memory Aids

"You have granted me life and favor,
And Your care has preserved my spirit."
JOB 10:12 NKJV

The topic of floral preservation became a family joke when I began invading my husband's workshop with bundles of flowers. During the day, his shop is dark, and ceiling joists offer elevations for suspending flowers. After awhile, Bob grew used to the presence of expired flora dangling over his table saw and jointer, but he noticed that visiting woodworkers looked askance at hanging hydrangeas and roses—even the female woodworkers! Bob and I arrived at a truce. His shop is now exclusively a birthplace for custom furniture, and our storeroom has become an equally good environment for parching florae.

Why dry flowers when you can grow or purchase fresh ones? Some people prefer the dried form; no watering is necessary. Dried flowers memorialize fresh ones and often commemorate the people or events where the live bouquets or corsages were used.

Shortly after my father was diagnosed with terminal cancer, he purchased three red roses to give my mother along with this note: "Three roses is a small thank you for a life together." Following his death, she displayed them, dried, in a glass box.

A tall antique pitcher in my living room holds a bouquet of dried pink roses saved on the day of my daughter's wedding.

Peach-colored birthday roses, a gift from my children, lie on the hearth.

An oak armoire in my guest room is topped with a bouquet of eighteen roses delivered to our home after my mother passed away.

Consider preserving flowers for both sentiment and decor. The process is easy.

Pick flowers just before their prime and remove foliage from the lower part of stems; some buds will open further while drying. Gather your flowers on non-rainy days after the dew burns off but before afternoon sun wilts the blossoms. Gather the flowers in small bunches bound with rubber bands; large bunches may mold.

Air-dry in a warm, well-ventilated, dark place. Avoid sunlight to preserve color. Hang flowers upside down on a laundry rack, from attic rafters (Martha Stewart's favorite drying location), or on a quilt rack where they will be undisturbed by people or pets. When fully dry, the stems will snap (usually within three to six weeks). Store your dried harvest in paper bags or boxes so they do not become dusty.

The whole point behind drying flowers is preservation. When the live form dies, a dried variety lingers, preserving a memory of the fresh. I look at my dried hydrangeas and recollect my huge bush with its globelike blooms. Memories help us stay in touch with the reality of the past. They preserve the beauty of a person or event.

The Root of the Matter: God, too, is in the business of preservation, and one of His methods is the marvelous gift of memory. God established Passover with the eating of lamb and bread dipped in bitter herbs to help the children of Israel remember when God delivered them from death and brutal slavery in Egypt. Jesus instituted Communion to help us remember that the sacrifice of His life delivered us from slavery to sin. Taking bread made from the grains of the garden and wine made from its grapes, Jesus said, "Whenever you eat this bread and drink this wine, remember that My body was given up and My blood was poured out for forgiveness of your sin" (Matthew 26:26–28 author's paraphrase).

The Fragrance of Praise: Thank You, God, for the faculty of memory that allows me to relive my favorite experiences.

Garden Tools: Recommended for Drying–
Perennials: *Acanthus spinosus, Achillea, Alchemilla mollis, Anaphalis, Aruncus dioicus,* astilbe, *Catananche.*
Annuals: winged everlasting, safflower, cockscomb, larkspur, globe amaranth, strawflower, pink paper daisy, statice.

Wildflowers: I remember the day my daughter came home from kindergarten and announced, "Guess what we planted? Dragonsnaps!" Jodie has heard me tell the story countless times and always shares this epilogue: "To this day, I can never remember if they are snap dragons or dragonsnaps!"

Gazing Around

"Whatever your hand finds to do,
do it with all your might."
ECCLESIASTES 9:10 NIV

Phyllis Northrop is the two-time past president of Associated Garden Clubs of Spokane. Though a resident of Washington State, she grew up in Hawaii watching her father tend exotic plants. "There was always an orchid on our lava rock fireplace," she said. Not surprisingly, one of her favored flowers is an Asiatic lily named 'Stargazer.' Blooming in mid-July, the crimson oriental hybrid is five feet tall, and its stalks sport six-inch blossoms.

Phyllis's intimate garden rates high in hospitality and originality. Four variously striped umbrellas shade tables and invite guests to come and sit. Among her flowers are monk's hood, *hydrangeas,* columbine, and Maltese-cross. Equally dazzling are some uncommon ornaments that are Phyllis's motif—eight colored gazing balls, nesting on various matching standards, coordinate with flowers in various spots of her garden.

Gazing balls date back to the Victorian Age. The eight- to twelve-inch glossy balls rest on pedestals or Corinthian pillars, accenting corners and groupings in her yard. A bronze ball blends with her yellow *Coreopsis,* and an emerald green ball complements an area where ivy is plenteous. Three silver balls, a wavy mauve, a starry white, and a royal blue ball draw gazers from flowers to balls, from balls to flowers.

Phyllis tells a story about a funny thing she overheard the day her garden was featured in a citywide garden tour. Among the thousand visitors strolling past her flowers and gazing balls, one of them exclaimed, "Oh, look at all the *grazing* balls!"

Phyllis herself is a gazer, in the most positive sense of the word. Long ago, a saying she heard became her practical philosophy for life. "Don't look back, don't look ahead, just look around." Rather than bemoaning the past, or living for the future, Phyllis has spent her life staying busy with things that catch her attention in the present—everywhere around her.

For six years she has served at her church by bringing altar flowers. Each of those 312 arrangements has been unique! Her philosophy of "looking around" enables her to originate her non-stop designs. This March, when fresh flowers were few, she gazed at a pile of pruned Hawthorne limbs, and suddenly she brightened with an idea for an arrangement. She tied together the dry sticks, tastefully spray-painted them gold, and garnished the bundle with dried Hydrangeas. Westminster Congregational parishioners were blessed again with a lovely one-of-a-kind centerpiece in their sanctuary because Phyllis chose to "look around."

An hour spent with this smiling lady would never make you suspect she's suffered her share of misfortune. But her philosophy of staying busy with things at hand has held her steady.

How wise it is to move beyond the past. And how futile it is to dwell only on the future. But how practical, like Phyllis, to stay current—to look around in the present and get to work with what's at hand.

The Root of the Matter: Some of the most memorable miracles recorded in the Bible were times when God asked man to notice what was in his hand. A small boy offered Jesus a few fish and over five thousand people were fed. When Moses needed to transport two million Israelites safely across the Red Sea, God told him to use the staff in his hand to divide the water so His people could walk to the other side. Whatever we need, God has placed it nearby—often within the reach of our hands.

The Fragrance of Praise: Dear God, I appreciate all You place under my nose to keep me occupied, useful, and happy.

Garden Tools: Place bulbs in firm contact with the soil. An air pocket between the base of the hole and the bottom of the bulb will prevent proper rooting and will cause the bulb to rot.

Wildflowers: One spring, Phyllis's daughter, Cynthia, asked her mother the name of some *Forsythia* trailing along the window ledge outside her bedroom. "What's that, Mother?" Phyllis answered, "It's 'For Cynthia'!"

Town Flower

Giving all diligence, add to your faith virtue;
and to virtue knowledge.
2 Peter 1:5

Some towns are known for their baseball fields and others as the birthplace of a famous person. Spokane, Washington is famed for its lilacs. Local garden historians record Spokane's lilac beginnings when Clara Denman came to Spokane Falls in 1883 with a slip of a Persian lilac.

The Spokane Floral Association, the oldest garden club in Washington State and the second oldest in the United States, formed in 1886. John Duncan, a former park board superintendent, visited

Rochester, New York, in 1912 and returned to Spokane with 128 lilac varieties. Soon, 174 lilacs were planted in two city parks. Duncan and horticulturist friends heartily encouraged the planting of lilacs in abundance. By 1933, the Floral Association and members of seven other garden clubs united as the Associated Garden Clubs of Spokane. Their primary objective became the promotion of Spokane as the Lilac City.

In May 1938, the clubs inaugurated the first Spokane Lilac Festival, a week-long event paying homage to the fragrant plumes of lilac. Huge bouquets flanked store entrances, and the lobby of the famous Davenport Hotel was a bower of lilacs. Three varieties, French, Persian, and Japanese, were on display at the flower show in the Spokane Art Center. Seven automobiles paraded downtown streets at noon. Aboard the only float were eight schoolgirls holding arms full of lilacs.

Festival enthusiasm grew. The second year, the American Legion Drill Team met arriving trains and buses to present lilacs to passengers. "Spokane's best when lilac drest" later became a slogan on a penny-a-piece festival sticker.

In succeeding years, lilac paintings, tours, pageants, style shows, a junior lilac parade, the Armed Forces Torchlight parade, a fine arts fair, a poetry contest, and distribution of lilac shoots evolved from those beginnings. A contest for the selection of a lilac queen was undertaken in 1942.

Faith Smith, then a college girl, was coincidentally downtown on the day of the first parade. She was taking art lessons held at the telegraph school where the flower show was located. She vividly recalls "Dr. Cowan's Peerless Dentists" audio truck playing "Lilacs in the Rain" and other lilac lyrics, as the parade rolled by.

Years later, Faith's own yard, a host to lilacs, was twice on the city garden tour. As past president, vice-president, and advisor of the Associated Garden Clubs, Faith wrote, "In a city that boasts a park system on a par with any worldwide, display gardens such as the Duncan Gardens, the Japanese Gardens, the Finch Arboretum, Riverfront Park, and small parks scattered in all neighborhoods, it is no small wonder that a flower, the lilac, dominates the wonderful week of Spokane's Lilac Festival."

Spokane has earned its namesake, the Lilac City. Lilacs remain its striking spring adornment and have become part of Spokane's virtue.

The Root of the Matter: Flowers and virtues are much alike. A flower can signify a place. Similarly, a salient virtue can characterize a person. Does your life evince a fragrant virtue? Portland, Oregon, is the city of roses; Spokane, the city of lilacs. Why not aspire to be characterized by your generosity or integrity?

The Fragrance of Praise: God of all virtues, I give You thanks for Your incomparable garden of graces.

Garden Tools: Be among those who grow the new lilac chosen in 1999 by the Spokane Lilac Society—double-pink, with both rounded and pointed petals, named the Spokane Lilac.

Wildflowers: "Gardens connect the years, thus, they are everlasting." PHYLLIS NORTHROP

The Rock

My soul finds rest in God alone;
my salvation comes from him.
He alone is my rock and my salvation;
he is my fortress, I will never be shaken.
PSALM 62:1–2 NIV

A gigantic rock in my backyard awakens countless memories and symbolizes powerful truths.

When an addition was built onto our home, excavators digging the basement unearthed an eight-by-three-by-five-foot boulder of granite. This ancient rock, speckled with mica, sparkles under sunlight. With its smooth and slanting table, it offers a perch for birds, a setting for snapshots, an observation site for cats and squirrels, a ledge for a beverage, a play center for children, and is an unfailing conversation piece. Its various functions chronicle events in our family's life.

My husband baits the rock with peanuts for squirrels and frequently rests pruning shears or a ball cap on its handy surface. If the cats need to be brushed, the rock becomes a grooming table. They scurry ahead and leap onto the rock when they see the wire brush in my hand.

The rock was a big attraction for our young daughter and son. Cautioned not to trample the cherry laurel at its south or the bishop's-weed at its north, they clamored atop and imagined themselves as pirate or princess. One winter, they built an igloo against one side of the rock. When my daughter was in seventh grade, the boulder became a stage for glamorous poses as she and a girlfriend photographed one another.

Not once have I thought, *If that rock wasn't there, I'd have room for a plot of azaleas or a few more rhodies*. Its contribution to our garden is as significant as the lawn or the fence.

I've invested in a few garden ornaments. A rabbit, a turtle and a frog, a sundial, a brass sign that reads "Kitty Crossing," and a small stone engraved with the promise, "As the garden grows, so shall the gardener." But the ornament I would last remove is our massive rock.

It speaks to me of strength, permanence, and availability—qualities of God. Transitory squirrels and migratory birds pausing there demonstrate how rocks are a resting place for the weary—the same refuge I find in God.

God is dependable and immovable—an edifice needed by every person, gardener or not. He's always present—too powerful to be shoved aside. He's always available—too kind to desert us. And He abides with us through all the stages of life, both the grievous and the gladsome.

The Root of the Matter: Wishing you had a resident rock in the midst of your garden? God, the Rock of Ages, is nearer than your own backyard. A garden rock may be the gift of nature. But the Rock of Ages is the gift of God Himself.

The Fragrance of Praise: Thank You, God, for the plain-spoken image of a rock, so clearly metaphorical of Your nature.

Garden Tools: For an alpine rock garden, select porous rocks like limestone, sandstone, shale, and tufa; these rocks absorb water, keeping roots cool and moist. Marble, basalt, and granite are preferable for desert rock gardens.

Wildflowers: Learn a spiritual lesson from alpine plants. They grow very close to a rock, enjoying extra water from runoff and a bit of shade from the rock's shadow.

Grace-Filled Performances

Be prepared in season and out of season.
2 TIMOTHY 4:2 NIV

D on't force it!" We've all heard the caveat. Like it or not, both human and plant life is filled with forced performances.

The glossary in the *Sunset Western Garden Book* gives this definition of the process called forcing: "hastening a plant along to maturity. . .or growing a plant to the flowering or fruiting stage out of its normal season. This is usually done by growing it in a greenhouse, where temperature, humidity, and light can be controlled."

When I recently visited my friend, Carolyn, I noticed a vase on her counter that held six arching wands of forsythia in yellow bloom.

My bush at home was not even budding. Curious, I asked, "Is your forsythia blooming already?"

"No, I forced these," she explained.

Her answer sent my thoughts running. Though I've never forced a bulb or cutting, I remembered the numerous times in life when I have been forced to bloom—to ignore the calendar of my emotions and conduct myself with flowerlike grace.

The word *force* makes us recoil. We dislike being shoved, coaxed, or prodded. But commitments that require us to be our best sometimes overlap with unexpected heartaches. Necessity demands that we bloom out of season—in the midst of a personal winter.

An author friend was slated for a reading shortly after the release of her first book. How much she had looked forward to that evening and the gathering of potential readers who would hang on the words of her novel. But two days prior, she learned that her college-age son had leukemia. Did she cancel her reading? The event had been scheduled months earlier. She stepped onto the podium, forced her smile, and spared her audience the facts of her personal life.

Frank had prepared six months for a business presentation. He was chosen to represent his company and herald their latest prototype at a trade show in another state. Just three days before the gathering, he received divorce papers from his wife of thirty-two years. The day of the show, he climbed aboard the jetliner determined to make a quality presentation. The enthusiasm he emulated for the new product was squeezed from his sense of responsibility, not from his heart.

We've all been there. Dinner guests ring the doorbell only moments after a phone caller relates sad news. We're forced to be cheerful hosts. Ten minutes before a dancer goes on stage, the director insults her. She forces the grace in every pirouette and manages to smile until the curtain drops.

How are these hard performances accomplished? How do we open our petals and emit a fragrance when life hits us broadside? Usually, by God's enabling. A greenhouse or other controlled environment will force a plant to bloom. Why not offer a prayer for self-control the next time you need grace to bloom?

The Root of the Matter: God doesn't force us into anything.
Instead, He leads us to green pastures and causes us to
lie down beside still waters. But, when the forces of
life do come against us, He has promised to be our

strong shield and ever-present help in time of trouble.

The Fragrance of Praise: Thank you, God, for Your sufficiency when my emotions are bankrupt.

Garden Tools: Amaryllis bulbs are frequently sold at Christmastime. If they are nurtured indoors near a sunny window for six to eight weeks, the lilies will bloom while outdoor gardens are still asleep under mulch or snow.

Wildflowers: Self-control is an act of disciplined strength.

Root-ing for Love

And I pray that you,
being rooted and established in love. . .
may be filled to the measure of all the fullness of God.
EPHESIANS 3:17, 19 NIV

She's really grounded, Mom." After only one week of baby-sitting young Courtney, my daughter could see that her cousin was rooted. Jodie's description struck me; it was a garden metaphor.

Plants are much like us, and we are much like plants. Without roots, we won't survive. It was plain to me what Jodie meant when she said her cousin was grounded. Most notably, Courtney had been loved, was capable of giving love, and recognized genuine love in others. Her adaptability and affectionate nature indicated emotional strength. She would not likely be blown away by the first fierce wind of adversity.

In the plant kingdom, roots operate underground, functioning in two ways. They anchor the plant against wind, gravity, and other above-ground movement while absorbing water and nutrients. Some roots store food to carry the plant through winter. Tiny root hairs, located behind the root tips, draw water into the larger root system. An inspection of a root ball reveals an amazing network of tentacles whose job is to brace the plant and to seek water and minerals necessary for the plant to manufacture food.

Fleshy taproots penetrate vertically and form delicate lateral roots that are sparse and finely branched. Some roots, like carrots and parsnips, are called swollen taproots; the enlarged roots serve as food storage organs. Fibrous roots are a fine network of many threadlike roots that emerge from the base of stems. The soil into which a plant's roots extend is called the root run.

A critical point when transplanting is to prepare a hole with lots of growing room for roots–both deep and wide. Holes should be two to three times larger than the root ball. Crumble the tightly packed soil that will surround the transplant; no clods, please. Then resettle the loosened dirt around the roots. A plant's new environment should make it easy for roots to begin their run, both vertically and laterally.

Most philosophies and religions assert that love, from others and for others, underlies stability. Thus, we spend much of our life rooting for love. The most deeply rooted people are those who are grounded in the assurance of God's unconditional love. Knowing we are loved empowers us to give love.

We can love imperfectly, expecting a return. Or we can root more deeply by loving others divinely, without reserve, and in spite of their uncomeliness, rank, color, or creed.

The Root of the Matter: Love does all the things for the human spirit that roots do for a plant. Love nourishes and stabilizes. It provides us with stores of patience, endurance, and long-suffering. Without love, we starve and topple. But founded in the love of God, we thrive and flourish and cheer the world.

The Fragrance of Praise: I'm so thankful, God! It matters not if my biological roots are illustrious or modest, for my spiritual roots are grounded in Your love.

Garden Tools: Rooting hormones, a chemical compound synthesized in powder or liquid form, can be introduced to new plants and transplants to encourage root production. A recommended amount is simply added to water in the planting hole.

Wildflowers: "A man's rootage is more important than his leafage."   WOODROW WILSON

Oh, No! Nomenclature!

"So do not fear, for I am with you;
do not be dismayed, for I am your God."
ISAIAH 41:10 NIV

I almost dismissed my ambition to be a writer, all because of nomenclature.

After attending a class taught by a best-selling author, I left overwhelmed. She was articulate, and her presentation was orderly. But her terms and abbreviations perplexed me. Terminology like market guide, simultaneous submissions, sidebar, clips, vanity publisher, IPRC, and SASE hindered my understanding of her lesson. I felt like a client who, with furrowed brow, asks the physician or attorney, "Now explain that to me in layperson terms."

Whatever discipline we pursue, we are met by nomenclature. I listen earnestly as my husband shares stories from work, but I seldom comprehend all he tells me—his conversations are punctuated with arcane phrases peculiar to engineering.

What do you suppose I found the least appealing about hobby gardening? More nomenclature. I quickly learned the meaning of soil pH (a measure of alkalinity or acidity in soils), biennials (plants that bloom the second year only and then die), soil amendment (adding improvements to poor soil), transpiration (leaf breathing), and dozens of other words. But the long, sophisticated, and classifying names given to plants put me off.

Carolus Linnaeus, the eighteenth century botanist, stepped in after Adam (of Adam and Eve) and devised a system using Latin for naming plants. First comes the name that designates the genus (always a noun), and second is the name of the species (always an adjective), a smaller grouping within the genus group. A third title is used by those less serious; it is the "common name." Allen Lacy, gardening columnist for the *New York Times,* calls this vernacular use the "giddy" name.

To give you an example of all three names, a plant informally called sea thrift bears the botanical name of *Armeria maritima*. The lovely and fragrant lilac is properly named *Syringa vulgaris,* though the "giddy" gardener would point to it and declare, "And over there are my lilacs!" Problems abound with common names. Often there are more than one for a particular plant and they may even be inaccurate—African violets are not really violets!

Long ago I decided to lay aside the intimidation of garden jargon in exchange for a bed of tulips. Don't cheat yourself out of smelling the fragrance of a carnation because you can't pronounce its botanical name *(Dianthus caryophyllus)!*

Now both a writer and a gardener, I'm glad I've leapt the nomenclature hurdle. Much to my own amusement, I find the vocabulary for both disciplines meaningful and fascinating.

The Root of the Matter: Bewilderment can be a hurdle that blocks our pursuit of new endeavors. Is there some obstacle besides nomenclature that is tripping you up? A fear, a memory, a doubt? Don't forego an ocean cruise because you never learned to swim, and don't miss out on experiencing God because you're puzzled by theological words. When you are baffled or lack wisdom, simply ask God to help you learn and to show you the truth.

The Fragrance of Praise: I thank You, God, that I don't have to know everything about something before I begin.

Garden Tools: Save the ID tag that comes with your plant. It will help you remember the plant's name, characteristics, care requirements, and appearance.

Wildflowers: A species' name may refer to the habitat it prefers, as in *pratensis* (meadows); a peculiar feature, like *acaulis* (no stems); the color of its flowers, as in *coccineus* (scarlet); its discoverer, as in *Gentiana farreri* (Reginald Farrer); or its size, as in *minutissimus* (really tiny).

Here a Bed, There a Bed

And let us not get tired of doing what is right,
for after a while we will reap a harvest of blessing
if we don't get discouraged and give up.
GALATIANS 6:9 TLB

One winter morning I shuffled through the untidy spectacle of my barren garden. Contemplating tasks that awaited me in each flower bed, I paused at a corner of dormant daylilies and kicked through fallen leaves beside a stretch of English ivy. I glanced at the iris bed and then northward at the daisy patch that lay covered under mounds of crusted snow. In obvious need of spring pruning, eight rosebushes stood as prickly and gangly as adolescents. I heard my garden calling in the February breeze, "Come tend me."

Feeling the chill, I hurried to the porch. The routines of garden duty suddenly felt heavy. "Don't come soon, springtime," I cautioned. "I'm not ready to help you reveal your glories."

Soon each sector would require hours of devoted care. Like a commander barking assignments at muster, my mind listed the chores ahead–spade, weed, fertilize, prune, mulch, plant, and transplant. The toil would be accomplished on bended knees and on some days when I would rather be reading a book. Happy anticipation was absent from this gardener's heart.

How had I done it year after passing year? A little at a time, of course. I solaced myself with a reminder: How do you tend a garden? One bed at a time.

I would indeed cooperate with the cycle of spring when the calendar turned to March. For a few days, one sector alone would become the most important parcel of earth in all the world. Tackling each small area, I would satisfy the special needs of the root-bound inhabitants emerging in each mini garden.

Hadn't I proved this method in other dimensions of my life? My one-thing-at-a-time approach is equally effective for responding to calls from church, school, children and friends, home, work, and recreation.

Neither life nor gardening need be overwhelming. By giving ourselves joyfully to the requirements and surprises of every day, we can approach each domain as if it were the most important, one duty at a time.

As winter eased into spring, my plants thrust through the hard ground and delighted my eyes. And God helped me, "the reluctant gardener," to push through my hardened unwillingness to labor patiently—here a bed, there a bed—for the rewards of a garden in bloom.

The Root of the Matter: Both our gardens and our lives will thrive if we invest our efforts in increments of commitment—one task at a time. And when responsibilities mount, just remember—God created the world one day at a time.

The Fragrance of Praise: I praise You, God, for the large recompense You grant for my small labors.

Garden Tools: Successful gardeners are record keepers. Purchase a small journal to keep in your garden apron or shed. (Not a fancy one; your entries will be made in garden gloves!) Make important and memorable notations—"Rhodies, trumpet vine, and roses need soil acidifiers," or, "The Japanese maple was fully red by 10/30/99." It's a diary you will cherish for both practical and sentimental reasons.

Wildflowers: Give the gift of an ivy plant to an engaged couple. Include a note: "Ivy has long been a symbol of fidelity in marriage. May this remind you of God's faithfulness to you and of your faithfulness to one another."

www.Garden.calm

When Jesus had spoken these words,
he went forth with his disciples across the Kidron valley,
where there was a garden, which he and his disciples entered. . . .
for Jesus often met there with his disciples.
JOHN 18:1–2 RSV

A commuter friend called me one day. "Hank and I rented a condo in the mountains. Good-bye, downtown and freeways!"

An insurance broker whose hobby is golf sent me this note written from a lake resort. "I'm enjoying a couple weeks here; I prefer the floating green to the office rush!"

An E-mail from a mother of four and her attorney husband

said, "I'm suffering from cabin fever and mother-mania. Jack and I are taking the kids to his mother's; ocean shores, here we come!"

A couple years ago, my husband and I were also among the depleted. Craving the serene, we didn't head for the mall, the seashore, or even the golf course. Where did we go for renewal? The tulip gardens near La Conner, Washington.

I've never had anyone tell me, "I have to get away from the garden!" When frenetic lifestyles drive people to retreat, they are more likely to flee to a garden, not from it.

Gardens are places of refuge. There we congregate with breeze-borne butterflies and scampering chipmunks. Soothing our senses is the pleasing angle of a tree, the feel of textured foliage, the scent of flowers and herbs, the taste of a spearmint leaf, or the song of a skylark.

God surely abides in gardens. He scooped Adam from the soil in the Garden of Eden and communed with him in that hallowed place. We sometimes forget that Jesus Christ chose a garden altar when he prayed in Gethsemane. And the greatest triumph of history transpired in the Garden of the Sepulcher where the crucified Son of God emerged eternal from a granite tomb.

Gardens will always be places of creation, surrender, and triumph. I've outlined formats for new books seated in a wicker chair beside the cherry laurel in my garden. I've wept my way to for-giveness strolling the grassy floor and been quickened by new dreams as my hands crumbled hardened earth.

Gardens nourish tranquility. Do you need a dose? In the gar-den sanctuary the gate is never locked. God's standing invitation is the same one inscribed on my garden gate. The painted letters spell "Welcome." Why not enter?

The Root of the Matter: Yours may be a formal garden or one as modest as an apartment balcony decorated with plants in terra-cotta pots. Maybe your only garden is the lily pond at a public park. Wherever it is, think of it as a habitat of God's presence. In a garden, calm awaits the harried, and God awaits the visitor.

The Fragrance of Praise: Thank You, God, for municipal parks that afford children and adults large expanses of gardens and arboretums.

Garden Tools: Considering a garden retreat? Why not visit the Butchart Gardens in Victoria, British Columbia (800 Benvento Ave., Brentwood Bay, Victoria, B.C., Canada V8M 1J8). The fifty acres of botanical gardens are one of the most popular destinations in the Northwest.

Wildflowers: "If you'd like a mind at peace, a heart that cannot harden, find a door that opens wide, upon a lovely garden." AUTHOR UNKNOWN

Garden Etiquette and the Dog Who Exhibited None

In everything a prudent man acts with knowledge.
PROVERBS 13:16 RSV

Lifetime owners of beloved felines, our family members are fervent cat lovers. However, like 20 percent of Americans, we once owned a dog. When I decided to become a serious gardener, I soon realized our malamute was better suited to Arctic trails than to my backyard. To my dismay, moist flower beds felt cooler on his massive chest than the lawn. He failed to recognize the difference between weeds and my fresh-set seedlings. He smashed young starts of would-be flora before they ever reached maturity. But Prince was family, so we tolerated his insulting lack of garden decorum.

When Prince died, we decided to restrict our pet population to cats. We later moved to another home where the perennials and shrubs were well established. By then, I, too, was well established in my hobby of gardening and was elated with the potential in my new yard. Did I mention that the kids still hankered for a dog?

One day my husband witnessed a man desert a beautiful malamute in the crook of a road. The poor animal stood confused, fearful, looking one way and then another. It was too much for my husband to ignore. The dog taxied home in the front seat of Bob's truck.

I returned from work the first evening after the dog's overnight stay. Eager to greet our new pet, I hurried to the back door. Through the window I spied him sprawled in the center of my daylily bed. Not one tall blade remained upright. My eyes moved toward the cover of English ivy along another fence line. It too was flattened. Here and there, geraniums lay broken, soft pink and coral petals pressed in the dirt. My honeysuckle, snapped at mid-height, was toppled in a bow toward the lawn—a bow of death.

I was speechless. Bob arrived home and after one sweep with his eyes, he joined me in disbelief at the destruction to our "well-established yard." We agreed on the dog's destiny. Perhaps a place in the country, on a farm, or by the sea! Bob returned the dog to our lakeside community, and neighbors offered to look after him.

Like every gardener, we had to settle on our priority. Even the kids admitted our canine boarder had to go. We still love dogs, but an unruly one may not be the best pet for a gardener. It's a choice between the *Dianthus* or the dog! We elected coneflowers over a canine. The cat, particularly, was relieved.

The Root of the Matter: It's a fact of life—some things are not compatible. A combination of even good things may not work simultaneously—like a small garden and a big dog. When weighing choices of all kinds, prudence may suggest you choose "either/or," but not "both." Asking the question "What is more important to me now?" will help you decide what to choose when desires conflict.

The Fragrance of Praise: Thank You, God, for the wisdom You offer when I must make tough choices.

Garden Tools: Make a rustic garden sign that lists a few codes of behavior for garden visitors. (1) "Tiptoe through the tulips." (2) "Please don't pick the flowers without asking." Add other rules that suit your setting and requirements.

Wildflowers: "I enjoy the garden for the Creator's personal bravura." MIRABEL OSLER

Surviving a Transplant

The LORD replied (to Moses),
"My Presence will go with you."
EXODUS 33:14 NIV

I try to select the ideal location for each newcomer to my garden. But every season, at least one new plant is noticeably misplaced and requires a transplant. A rosebush may be crowded. "This is a prickly situation," she complains. A *Weigela* might need more sunshine. "Please, warm me up," he shivers. Sometimes I rearrange a grouping of flowers merely for artistic reasons. Making geographical changes is a common garden activity.

Transplanting is traumatic for plant life and can be fatal if not accomplished with sensitivity. Some plants endure movement better than others, but all suffer a measure of shock when they are dug up and resettled. Blooms may go limp and foliage may droop.

Two simple things contribute to success–preparation and aftercare. Both processes minimize plant stress.

First, adequately prepare the traveler by watering it. Allow enough time for life-giving water to reach the tips of growth. Don't make the move during the warmest hours of the day. Ready the new location before removing the transplant to avoid prolonged exposure of the root system to sunrays, chill, or wind. Be sure the soil of the new bed is not impoverished, and loosen soil so roots have easy movement as they reach outward in their new home.

Secondly, observe the plant in its new locale for several days. The success or failure of the move will be easy to detect. Tend to any of its obvious needs. A neighboring plant may be tickling its foliage; snip it. The water furrow you formed may have a leak; rebuild it.

Like a garden transplant, we, too, must make transitions and adjustments. Education choices may transplant us to a college far from home. Career advances transport us to new cities. Family transitions change us from full nesters to empty nesters, from homemakers to breadwinners. The reckless intrusion of death may move our status from married to single, from parenthood to childless. Such transitions can be far more shocking to our minds, emotions, and bodies than the movement of a daisy from the front yard to the back.

How do we survive those tough transitions that pull us from our firmly rooted zones? Once again, the answer is preparation and aftercare.

We cannot foresee the future, but we can prepare by cultivating the daily practice of leaning on God. After every transition, heed the cry of your emotions. Address your need for rest, adjustment, and time. Don't neglect the tender aftercare.

The Root of the Matter: The gardener's goal for a transplant is that it thrives—not merely survives. When the transitions of life shove us from one place to another, God's goal for us is no less. A new location, whether it is emotional, relational, or geographical, may not feel like a better one—at least not at first. So be assured— God makes every move with you.

The Fragrance of Praise: I praise You, God, for Your unfailing commitment to abide with me wherever You guide.

Garden Tools: Dig a hole wide enough for the root ball of your transplant. To estimate the size of the root ball, calculate like this: The ball will measure about twelve inches wide for every inch of trunk diameter. Thus, a shrub whose stem is two inches in diameter will have a root ball at least twenty four inches wide.

Wildflowers: People are like plants: The older they grow, the less they like to move!

The Cutting Edge

"I am the true vine, and my Father is the gardener.
He cuts off every branch in me that bears no fruit,
while every branch that does bear fruit he prunes
so that it will be even more fruitful."
JOHN 15:12 NIV

One spring I grew impatient waiting for my husband to dig out a shrub. Disenchanted with the misshapen climber, I decided something different would be preferable in that spot. I grabbed my shears on an impulse and amputated every stem at ground level.

Summer progressed, and the barely visible evergreen bittersweet was forgotten. Much to my surprise, though, my radical pruning was not fatal. The hardy shrub was neither daunted nor stunted. By fall, new growth testified to its livelihood. The following spring I trained its new branches in graceful arches up the chimney.

The experience with my shrub reminds me of a painful episode in my life as a young missionary in Africa. After battling malaria for fourteen months while teaching in Kenya, I reluctantly conceded to broken health and returned to the United States. My debilitating illness and an assault on my faith leveled me.

I was confused over God's intentions. Seized often by nausea, I also wrestled with the challenge of recurring attacks of malaria. My dismay over the curtailment of a life goal buffeted me. I felt like a razed shrub.

But in God's time, I experienced a renewal that matched the recovery of my shrub. The cycle of revival in the plant world is symbolic. It reminds us of the promise of resurrection that awaits in a coming season.

Words from the Book of Job became my emotional lattice, and my healing began: "There is hope of a tree, if it be cut down, that it will sprout again, and that the tender branch thereof will not cease" (14:7).

Emotional and physical recovery is sometimes as gradual as the slow unfurling of a tiny new leaf. But the love of parents, the counsel of ministers, the care of physicians, and months of rest healed my brokenness. One day I realized I was sprouting! Tender shoots of joy, faith, and physical strength had grown under the sunshine of God's faithfulness. It was springtime once again!

The Root of the Matter: Gardeners realize the value of reshaping, retraining, and controlling the contours of a plant. Can we not then trust God when He clips away at us with divine secateurs? He intends only to enhance those whom He prunes. How much more will we flourish when we are sheared by the expert skills of the Master Gardener!

The Fragrance of Praise: Thank You, God, for roots that keep me anchored when You prune my wayward limbs.

Garden Tools: The pruning of trees more than ten to fifteen feet tall should be assigned to professional arborists.

They are trained and equipped to do the job properly and safely. For information about tree pruning, visit this web site: http://www.isa-arbor.com

Wildflowers: "If rivers come out of their icy prison thus bright and immortal, shall not I too resume my spring life with joy and hope?"   HENRY D. THOREAU

Growing Perfume

May the God of hope fill you with all joy
and peace as you trust in him.
ROMANS 15:13 NIV

Each time I spray a cool mist of my favorite cologne, I borrow a fragrance from a garden somewhere in the world. Though one of my perfumes is named after a boulevard in France, the scent itself is the fragrance of violets. My backyard boasts one bed that grows the perfumes of lavender, lemon balm, sage, and peppermint, sensual contributions to the garden.

Did you ever stop to realize how the perfumes with which we scent our bodies are grown? The agreeable odors of plants are found in the leaves, as in sage, thyme, and mint; in the bark, as in cinnamon and cassia; in the wood, as in cedar and sandalwood; in the flower petals, as in the rose and violet; in the seeds, as in anise and caraway; and even in the roots, as in the orris.

While temporarily in a budget crunch, I learned even more about growing perfume. Our money was tight and my cologne bottles were empty. I felt unjustified apportioning any of our minimal funds for the purpose of smelling good.

One morning I reached for a bottle of my favorite fragrance only to remember the fancy flask was dry. Wistful, I heard the Lord whisper near the ear where I lavish perfume. He spoke gently. "I want you to wear Joy."

What a novel suggestion. "I'm to wear Joy!" I agreed it was a gracious scent too often neglected by women busied with child care, career demands, and other commitments. My own present challenge was merely financial. Would I accept God's brand of fragrance and put on joy?

In an act as deliberate as reaching for a decanter of "Gardenia," pressing an atomizer, and pointing it below my ear, I donned a smile and resolved to let joy touch everyone I contacted that day. Rather than breathe the sweet essence of perfume, others would inhale my spirit of joy. I purposed to say affirming things to people, and when the trite question was posed, "And how are you today?" I would answer, "Wonderful, thank you!"

My imagination took me further. I envisioned a perfume bar displayed with an array of elegant vials variously named Peace, Kindness, Encouragement, and Humor. Each one was tagged with this explanation: "Priceless. God has purchased these graces for you; simply apply and enjoy."

Most man-made perfumes are evanescent—fleeting at best. But virtues of the heart endure like no additive concocted by perfumeries. And they are free to anyone willing to imitate the character of God.

The Root of the Matter: Why not permeate your surroundings with the traits of God's nature? Wear His attributes like you would a perfume. Believe me, people will begin asking, "What fragrance are you wearing?"

Just answer, "Oh, it's called 'Joy' and the Maker is divine!"

The Fragrance of Praise: How amazing, God, that we begin feeling joy as soon as we act it out!

Garden Tools: English lavender (also pink, white, and blue), a fragrant perennial, is easy to grow in any well-drained loam or sandy soil in full sun. To use in sachets, cut flower clusters or strip flowers from stems just as color shows; dry in a cool, shady location.

Wildflowers: Grasse, France, is the center for the natural perfumery industry. The culture of flowers for perfumes is located in Turkey, Bulgaria, India, and Syria.

Naturalizing

But when the kindness and love of God our Savior appeared,
he saved us, not because of righteous things we had done,
but because of his mercy.
TITUS 3:4–5 NIV

Bill, listen to this!" Colleen spun around as she turned to read from a garden catalog. "You don't need a professional to design a layout for a striking display of spring color. For an informal garden, simply face the direction you want to plant, and toss a mixture of bulbs onto the ground. Wherever they fall, dig a hole the depth of two-and-one-half times the diameter of the bulbs, and set them in the ground."

Colleen was ebullient! "This I can do! Just throw them in the beds and let them fall where they may! Wow, Billy, let's do it! I get tied in knots thinking about where and how to arrange a hundred bulbs, but this sounds easy! It's called naturalizing."

Bill's tender heart bowed to his wife's enthusiasm. There was still time to order the selection of daffodils, crocuses, tulips, hyacinths, and alpines. Colleen would reserve a Saturday for planting to insure their investment resulted in the setting of all one hundred bulbs.

"Scattering the bulbs will be a ball, Billy. I'll plant fifty and you plant fifty." Bill smiled and agreed, but secretly, it wasn't his dream come true. For Colleen, it was that precisely.

Spring after spring she had wished for early blooms in her yard. But every fall, she felt inadequate. *How should I space them? Shall I put six in a row? No, that's so tidy. Maybe only three? But that might look skimpy. Shall I follow the borderline of the bed? No, that's unnatural. Should I plant them in a drift? How many would I need for a drift? What if I confuse the bulbs and plant pink blooms beside orange blooms? Not a good combination.* The more she mused, the more doubtful she felt about the outcome. Thus, for twenty-five years, she deprived herself of the glory of spring color.

Until last year! One cool autumn morning, two adults at work, behaving more like children at play, tossed bulbs in random places.

Near the fence, beside a shrub, in a corner bed, they cast the bulbs in woodsy style. Equipped with a trowel and a sack of bulb food, they spent a couple of hours digging in the dirt.

The following spring, they thrilled to the bounteous reward of color and marveled as they remembered the carefree method that brought them such beauty.

The Root of the Matter: Colleen gets just as excited explaining how her experience with the bulbs parallels a spiritual misconception that once restrained her. "Just like my frustration about perfect placement of the bulbs, I used to think I had to do everything for God 'just right.' What freedom it was the day I relaxed about bulb planting and just did it! Equally as freeing was the revelation that God doesn't expect perfection in my efforts to obey Him." Smiling as brightly as a yellow daffodil, she said, "I no longer have a colorless yard, and I'm no longer stymied in my service to God."

The Fragrance of Praise: Dear God, Creator of woods and gardens, I praise You for the casual beauty of nature.

Garden Tools: Don't combine tulips with daffodils in a vase. The sappy secretion of cut daffodils is especially harmful to tulips. Allow daffodils to be in a vase alone for at least six hours before mixing them with other flowers.

Wildflowers: Avoid the grave error of doing nothing because you fear it will be less than perfect.

Horticulture Heaven

And we know that all things work together
for good to those who love God.
ROMANS 8:28 NKJV

In 1904, on a hill above Tod Inlet on Vancouver Island, lived Jenny Foster Butchart. She was the daughter of a successful seed and commission merchant, and her husband, Robert, was a manufacturer of Portland cement. His first limestone quarry was located on the 130-acre tract where he built their house.

When the limestone was depleted, his wife hated the bleak 3½-acre hole in view of their home. One day her horticultural passions seized on an idea. In her own words, "Like a flame, the limestone pit burst into imaginary bloom. A flame for which I shall ever thank God." She planned to turn the dismal pit into a sunken garden. It was, indeed, visionary. A friend commented to Jenny, "Even you would be unable to get anything to grow in there."

Her inspiration would need feet. Jenny hired laid-off cement employees eager to find work. Thousands of tons of topsoil arrived by horse and cart as Jenny changed an abyss into a paradise. To cover the steep quarry walls, her workers planted ivy. Next, paths descending at a gentle grade were cut into the garden. The transformation became apparent when annuals, rare shrubs and trees, and *Meconopsis,* the Himalayan blue poppy, took root in the once-barren hole.

Jenny did some of the work herself, one day laboring for twelve hours. Biographer Dave Preston tells the story of Jenny being "dangled down fifty-foot cliffs in a basketwork bosun's chair, while she tucked tiny pieces of ivy into (rock) crevices." After two years, the garden was unveiled for the public.

A rose garden, a Japanese garden, a formal Italian garden, water gardens and fountains, including the "soda" fountain, were added in later years. A crater in the middle of the quarry was lined and filled with water to make a peaceful lake, stocked with trout and surrounded by a carpet of flowers and grass. Thousands of tourists were drawn by the growing reputation of the extraordinary gardens.

Jenny's signature was not only her gardens but also her hospitality. She exhibited great enthusiasm for sharing her paradise with others. In 1915, she served eighteen thousand cups of tea to visitors, just for the pleasure of their company.

Today, over ninety years since Jenny's vision "of imaginary bloom," the sunken garden is still the centerpiece of the famed Butchart Gardens in Victoria, British Columbia. More than one million people visit each year.

The Root of the Matter: Jenny's response to a problem and her vision for change are typical of those who face difficulty with an eye for opportunity. I can look out my window and hate what I see, or I can put on work gloves and change the view. Jenny could not remove the quarry but she could change it into a garden! Take heart! Big troubles often resolve in big blessings.

The Fragrance of Praise: Thank You, God, for the promise that good things can come from bad.

Garden Tools: Though we may dislike the work of planning, the garden with the best outcome results from thoughtful design. Books are available that address the specific subject of landscape possibilities.

Wildflowers: The words of Thomas Campion (d. 1620) could be said of Jenny Butchart: "There is a garden in her face, where roses and white lilies grow."

Message in a Rose

"Speak, for your servant is listening."
1 SAMUEL 3:10 NIV

A careful rosarian, I snipped the long stem at the recommended angle after discovering the choice flower. Lifting the lavender bloom to my nose, I stole a deep breath of scent from the first rose of spring. I carried the rose indoors as tenderly as though I were bearing my own sweet mother in my arms. It was Memorial Day, and this single bloom would garnish her grave marker.

Only days before, Mom had passed away and I was still numb from the drain of grief and the consequent exhaustion. Concentration on Mom's funeral preparations and a brunch in my home afterwards halted all attention to my garden.

Among my fourteen rosebushes, one of the three in a bed with southern exposure is usually the first to bloom. "Fire King," a brilliant red-orange floribunda, sits between "Queen Elizabeth," a true pink grandiflora, and "Blue Ribbon," the soft lavender variety—my only rosebush in bloom that day.

Had it been any other day or any other rose, there would have been no significance to that early burst of spring blossom. But purple was my mother's favorite color.

One of the first colors my toddler son learned to pronounce was "poo-pull." In preschool years, he'd often notice something purple and say, "Mammer would like that, Mommy; it's poo-pull!" Purple was Mom's trademark. Much to the chagrin of lakeside neighbors, even the family's summer cabin was painted lavender—with hot pink trim. Her car was a deep wine, as close as she could come to purple. She wore amethyst jewelry, donned her guest-room beds with purple velvet bedspreads, and cherished her own lavender rosebush, "Sterling Silver." She was laid to rest in purple gemstone earrings, a purple silk blouse, and purple leather slacks—this lady was always in vogue. Lavender roses draped her casket, and purple pansies decorated the petit fours served at her memorial brunch.

That morning when I stepped outdoors to look more closely at the only blooming rose in all my garden, it was a reverent moment. God seemed to be speaking for Mom. She, who had loved her Savior as passionately as she loved His electric color purple, was alive–in heaven. Her spirit was as fresh as the lavender rose.

God often speaks to us in garden homilies. A towering treetop reminds us of His majesty. A vine teaches us to cling to Him. A desert flower tells us that He's present when our heart is parched and our emotions are scorched. But do we hear Him? Through a lavender rose He said, "She's with Me." Every expression of kindness, every gift and provision, and every flower that blooms is a messenger of God.

The Root of the Matter: God is unlimited in the ways He speaks. Sometimes He uses our circumstances. The Book of Acts tells of many situations when God spoke to individuals through other people. The Old Testament book of Numbers, chapter 22, records a time when God spoke through a donkey to the disobedient prophet Balaam! Elijah, another prophet, heard God through a still, small voice. God will use whatever He can to communicate His love; we need only to watch and listen.

The Fragrance of Praise: God of infinite expression, thank You for the endless means by which You speak.

Garden Tools: Water modern roses several times a week to a depth of three inches. "Old garden roses" need watering once a week. Use drip irrigation or a soaker hose to avoid wetting the foliage and encouraging black spot. If an overhead sprinkler is used, water in the morning so foliage dries quickly.

Wildflowers: Introduced in 1954, the first grandiflora rose was "Queen Elizabeth." It represents the best characteristics of its parents, hybrid tea and floribunda roses.

Sharing the Yield

Each man should give what he has decided in his heart to give,
not reluctantly or under compulsion, for God loves a cheerful giver.
2 CORINTHIANS 9:7 NIV

When Sali Combelic began sharing her peonies in the small community of Peaceful Valley, she made a discovery. "My mother's heart is my own," she said.

"More impressive than Mom's spectacular acre of flowers and vegetables, was how she gave her plants to anyone who admired them," Sali said. "I learned from her that sharing is the spirit of gardening."

Sali earned a degree in horticulture and then sought a fine arts and architecture degree at a college where she managed the campus nursery and landscaped the grounds.

While she was a grower at the Institute of Biochemistry, a fame-seeker under whom Sali worked lost sight of the heart of gardening while striving for a Nobel Prize. "He almost squelched the spirit of my gardening heritage," she said. One day, she left.

Next, she managed the third largest mail-order perennial business in the West. With the goal of starting her own peony nursery, she began buying varieties for herself. Six years later, she had established her own peony farm on a corner lot near her house.

"Peony lovers in Peaceful Valley helped me recover my mother's protocol of sharing," she added. "Community walkers, joggers, and gazers passed by. One day I said to an admirer, 'That one's called Dainty Lass. It'll be in a can on the sidewalk for you tomorrow.' It felt natural to model my mother," said Sali. Similar incidences kept happening. "Soon I realized that sharing my garden was as good as viewing it."

A photographer and her daughter toured the vicinity one afternoon and noticed volunteer horse chestnut seedlings speckling Sali's paths. The photographer owned ten acres of sparsely treed land. "Let's dig these up!" Sali offered. Slack-jawed with amazement, the photographer and daughter accepted and helped Sali uproot one hundred or more eight-inch seedlings. When Sali needed a portrait shot for her business card, guess who offered to do the photography?

Though Sali expects nothing in return, many give a thank you–like a bag of sticky notes and other desk items. One morning, she found a sack of fresh bread at her front door. Another anonymous giver left ten iris rhizomes.

Sali enjoys living among the 140 homes in her riverside community. After the Spokane fire in 1889, Peaceful Valley was a shantytown of blue-collar workers rebuilding the city. Today it is a mix of eighty percent low-income residents, and twenty percent owners who are restoring the shotgun-style Victorian homes. In 1989, Sali bought her house in the cozy district and later purchased the nearby lot where she planted her white, pink, red, and species peonies.

"In Peaceful Valley, we support one another and ask questions last. For example, a successful resident-poet went door-to-door collecting money to help a strapped neighbor pay her mortgage. That's the kind of 'do-something' caring that happens here," said Sali. Originally, Sali's peony lot was on another corner near her home. The owner agreed to let her plant there. When the owner died, the heirs gave Sali "twenty minutes to get off the property." Seeing Sali in tears, a watching neighbor rushed over. In five minutes a handful of neighbors arrived with shovels. The informal team salvaged two-thirds of her plants.

For Sali, giving has become more than a gardening principle. Presently, she's living in her garage, which she had plumbed and wired, so her sister and family can live in her house. Also a full-time realtor, she sometimes accepts smaller commissions to help out a buyer. "It's the spirit of gardening," she said. But it touches all areas of Sali's life.

The Root of the Matter: Giving is like a law of nature. Similar to cause and effect, when you give, there's always a return. God is the Divine Reciprocator.

The Fragrance of Praise: Thank You, God, for a heart to give and for the bonus of returns.

Garden Tools: Peony flower types are called single, Japanese, anemone, semi-double, semi-rose, rose, and bomb.

Wildflowers: Many nurseries still emulate the spirit of gardening by adding a free plant to every order.

The Family That Gardens Together

*We worked night and day, laboring and toiling. . .
in order to make ourselves a model for you to follow.*
2 THESSALONIANS 3:8–9 NIV

When wheat and barley farmer, Jim Leifer, was considering a second enterprise, he suggested two possibilities to his wife. "Honey, we can raise pigs or grow irises."

"But pigs smell!" Janet winced.

"So do irises!" countered Jim.

The couple opted for the sweet smell of flowers. Soon after, they purchased Austin Morgan's thirty-five-year-old iris business. In 1990, they began moving two thousand varieties of bearded iris to the 1,690-acre farm they lease. Five years later, they were ready to market the rhizomes nationwide.

Last year, two thousand people visited the Iris Test Garden during the blooming season. They walked the rows, lunched at picnic tables, and tasted a bit of farm life. Tourists admired plant residents like "Red Tornado," "Popsicle," and "Capricious," while a family guide commented on the iris design. Standards, (three upright petals), falls (three lower petals), hafts, style arm, flare, plicata, and amoena are words understood by iris fanciers. The Leifers' catalog lists thirty words describing the plant.

Janet and Jim are high-energy folks with enthusiasm for more than irises. Janet is active at church, cares for two daughters and a son, and has done foster care for twenty-five children over the past eight years. Their web site lists business hours as "dawn to dusk." Janet fits homemaking in between, though she said, "We often eat buffet style." Janet was never a gardener, yet Jim contends she's the most meticulous weeder in the family. Her leisurely weed-hunting strolls (no hands and knees weeding necessary) are among her best times, she said. "Our lifestyle doesn't buy us luxuries, but when I look at the irises, the beauty of our farmland, and my extraordinary family, I realize how rich I am."

Jim, too, is a happy man. "I am blessed with the most wonderful and energetic wife who is my partner in business and my best friend in life." Jim is also a federal crop insurance agent. He has a master's degree in soils and agronomy. "We use the best-known conservation practices to maintain and improve our soils," he says.

What makes the iris garden increasingly successful? Perhaps it's the specialized fertilizer Jim has concocted, but the Leifers credit the family as a whole. "We couldn't do this without the cooperation of the kids–they're our biggest blessings!" the Leifers affirm.

The children plant, weed, take phone orders, and greet visitors. These kids don't vacation in Disneyland during spring break. They're raking dead iris leaves into piles to burn. In July, they spend two weeks digging up the rhizomes and shipping orders. Even seven-year-old Logan helps by clipping leaves from the iris.

Fifteen-year-old Larissa said, "My favorite time to work is in the evening, in the summer, by myself. After a long day, that is really relaxing." The children are paid for their labors. The girls save for college and buy all their clothes. Thirteen-year-old Litney is the "pacer or goal" for other youth whom they sometimes hire. "I like it when just my mom and dad and sister and brother are in the field. There's no phone, no television or radio, and we can talk about anything and everything."

Jim said, "I truly believe the Lord directed us toward the iris nursery as a way of bringing our family close together."

Whether cultivating irises or raising pigs, working together adds a sweet scent to family life.

The Root of the Matter: Much is said about the value of families playing together. But families who work together also experience a union of hearts while toiling side by side. Working as a family teaches children responsibility and rewards parents in support and pride.

The Fragrance of Praise: Dear God, thank You for the fragrance of fellowship in the midst of our labors.

Garden Tools: Irises should be planted twelve to fourteen inches apart within a row, and rows should be separated at least twenty-four inches.

Wildflowers: Visit the Iris Test Garden web site: http://www.iristg.com

The Dirt-Clod Sermon

Break up your unplowed ground;
for it is time to seek the LORD,
until he comes and showers righteousness on you.
HOSEA 10:12 NIV

Pastor Brent Harris likes to preach and likes to plant. You might guess he does a lot of praying in his vegetable rows. But you might not guess his dirt clods go to church.

Four gardens, three of which he was forced to abandon, haven't faded his green thumb. In fact, time spent rototilling, irrigating, and weeding have given him a harvest of both produce and sermons. His green thumb and index finger assist each other. One digs in the brown soil and the other points the spiritual way.

His best-ever sermon was born in his garden. "I'll never forget 'Dirt-Clod Sunday,'" his parishioners still say. "The lesson you demonstrated changed my life."

At that time, Brent and his wife were renting a duplex in Cupertino, California. Determined to have a garden plot, Brent settled on the only conceivable spot–a four-by-fifteen-foot strip of soil with adequate exposure to sun.

Though equipped with hoe and trowel, tools designed for typical soil, Brent was in for a surprise. A few firm downstrokes with the long-handled hoe, and he concluded that this parcel of earth had never been home to vegetation. The ground was so hard, the point of his hoe sank only a quarter inch. He whaled on, next with a pickax and other tools not intended for gardens! A sunburn and a quart of perspiration later, he had only raised some dust.

"Brent, yuh gotta flood it," a friend advised. "Lay the hose in that area and let the water run slowly for several hours. You'll have no trouble loosening the soil after that." The recommendation made sense, but the results were pathetic. Gallons of water soaked only a half-inch deep. Now he was forced to labor in a puddle. Convinced there was no easy way, he continued with his previous methods of brute force.

That evening, as he shared his frustration with his wife, a powerful truth struck him like the pickax. "Honey, that soil is just like people! Our hearts are sometimes hard. Unless we do the humbling work of repentance and cultivate a tender heart, nothing God does soaks in. He floods us with mercies, provision, and promises of Scripture, but we don't respond. Impervious, we wonder, Where's God?"

There was his next sermon topic. He'd even take a dirt clod to church and use it for an object lesson.

That Sunday morning, Brent captured the full attention of his congregation. He poured two quarts of water over the clod, which he'd put in a bowl. By the end of the sermon, it looked saturated. "But friends, look further," he said. He broke open the clod. "Inside is a dry mass."

The congregation was deeply moved. Silent prayers rose, *Am I like that, God?* Many wept and asked forgiveness for the impenetrable condition of their hearts.

A weekend later, Brent added amendments to the soil at his duplex and planted his seeds. Soon after, he was called to pastor another church. When the garden was ripe, new tenants harvested his crop. "But there was a spiritual compensation," Brent said. "The results of the dirt-clod sermon were a better harvest than anything my vines or stalks could ever have produced."

The Root of the Matter: Allowing God to break up the hard soil of our hearts is only a beginning. To keep our hearts tender, we must constantly be watered by the truths of God's Word.

The Fragrance of Praise: Dear God, thank You for a bountiful harvest and a pliable heart.

Garden Tools: Choose tools with these handle attachments: solid-strap—the metal tongue extends from the blade and is screwed onto the handle; and solid-socket—the handle inserts into a closed metal tube.

Wildflowers: Lois Johnson tells of the time her mother asked her to fry the potatoes. "Add a sliced onion," she instructed. The next day her mother couldn't find the hyacinth bulb she'd left on the kitchen counter. Lois had mistaken it for an onion!

Garden Medicine Nourishes Faith

*"I have come into the world as a light,
so that no one who believes in me should stay in darkness."*
JOHN 12:46 NIV

For ten years, Sister Michelle Holland, a Sister of Providence, dreamed of a center where the ill, their caregivers, friends, and family could come for spiritual support and repose. In 1998, the Sisters of Providence donated their convent to Sacred Heart Medical Center. Eventually, that space became the Providence Center for Faith and Healing, thus fulfilling Sister Michelle's vision. In May 2000, the center celebrated its first birthday. Among its various ministries, a large garden plays no small part.

Sacred Heart Medical Center, staffed by 3,800 workers, is located on the same grounds; its front doors are only a few steps away. The Providence Center enhances the Catholic hospital's mission by integrating faith and health. By offering both a sacred and a scientific environment for healing, Sacred Heart has become a national model.

The Providence Center's lush garden, bordered on three sides by brick buildings, is a sanctuary of ponds, paths, shrubs, and flowers. Lavender azaleas in spring, yellow *Potentilla* in summer, and red maple leaves in fall invite those whose lives may feel colorless to rest in God's presence. Two gates designed of rusted ironwork swing open to pathways. Several sculptures, man's handiwork, blend with the surrounding plant life of God's handiwork.

"I continue to notice a variety of services the garden offers the hurting," said employee Janet Sanders. "Parents who lost a child were escorted to the garden where they could find privacy and seek solace. Five memorial services were held in the garden. Staff from the hospital's psychiatric unit brought a group of troubled child patients there and led them in gamelike exercises to promote trust. Friends and family who grow weary in waiting rooms often take a break in garden sunlight to dispel shadows of doubt, discouragement, and fear."

A focal point in the garden is the *Lucenarius,* a Latin word meaning lamp stand. Its eternally lit candle represents Christ's light to the world and our call to be that light to one another. On Mondays, chaplains of many faiths gather at the lamp stand to remember those who were born and those who died during the week, and to pray for patients, their relatives, physicians, and other medical staff. The *Lucenarius* was built when memorial funds were donated in honor of the Pearsons, a local family who perished in a 1999 airline crash.

The Providence Center is a devoted place available to any who seek God and spiritual nourishment in a time of suffering. The center's brochure promises, "Here, even the smallest grain of faith is nurtured." Some of the nurture transpires in the resource library, some in a support group, some in rooms for private meditation, and some in the garden.

In many cases, faith is welcomed in the recovery process. Health-care studies prove that faith in God has a favorable effect on coping with grief and chronic illness, on survival rates, and on healthy living in general. Forty-eight percent of patients desire to pray with their doctors or other health providers. Prayer is commonly offered in hospitals and churches. But could there be any more serene place for praying than in a garden?

The Root of the Matter: Is your heart or body broken? Find
a garden and talk honestly to God. Even without a
Lucenarius, you can experience His light. Jesus Christ
proclaimed, "I am the Light of the world." Only His
brightness can penetrate the hollow darkness of physical suffering, heartache, and loss.

The Fragrance of Praise: God of light, You illumine both
happy days and troublesome nights.

Garden Tools: Testify to your faith with garden ornaments—
a redwood cross, a candle lantern placed on driftwood
or a tree stump, a prayer engraved on a small sign, or
a molded ceramic of praying hands.

Wildflowers: "Faith burns in the hearts of most Americans,
a faith yearning for expression in clinic offices and
hospital surgical suites just as it does in quiet moments
of prayer at home or in a place of worship."

DALE MATTHEWS, M.D.

Firstfruit Felicitations

In everything give thanks:
for this is the will of God.
1 THESSALONIANS 5:18

Karen balanced the bottom of the brilliant red pepper between thumb and forefinger. A prize pick! Smacking her lips, she savored an imaginary foretaste of its sweet flavor. *Look what came out of this garden!* She restrained the desire to shout. That year, the Wingate family would begin a copycat tradition of gratefulness modeled after an Israelite feast.

To Karen's pleasure, and as much to her surprise, it had been a fertile year. Surveying the remainder of her September garden, she admired plump beefsteak tomatoes–not yet sampled by insects–rosebushes dressed in polka dots of pastel bloom, and drooping pepper plants laden with an abundant crop. "I could take no credit," Karen was quick to say. "Our family had anticipated a small harvest. A dry spring and an unseasonably wet and cool summer lessened our hopes for large yields."

Nonetheless, the garden was an enviable cornucopia of mature crops. Even the neighbors noticed the colorful raiment of flowers and vegetables clothing Karen's garden. One had asked, "What's your secret? Your rosebushes are extraordinary!" Jokingly, she answered, "Botch your pruning." The thorny bushes had thrived despite her hack-and-slash technique. What more could she say? She had planted, watered, pruned (so to speak), and harvested, but if she'd taken credit in the past, this year, God deserved the praise.

That fall, the appreciation Karen felt turned her thoughts to an ancient Hebrew celebration. God had given instructions through Moses. "When you enter the land I am going to give you and you reap its harvest, bring to the priest a sheaf of the first grain you harvest" (Leviticus 23:10 NIV). The Israelites were required also to bring an offering of new grain fifty days afterwards. On that holy day, they worshipped, sacrificed, abstained from work, and celebrated.

How interesting that God requested the firstfruits, not the last.

Karen commented, "Which do I yearn for? The first tomato of the season or the last? Given a choice of one only, I'd choose the first ripe produce over the last." Not only are firstfruits the reward for tilling, weeding, and watering, they are harbingers of the remaining harvest.

The Wingates decided to instate their own family feast to commemorate their garden harvests. "After picking a first tomato, the first tender leaves of lettuce, or that first red pepper, we conduct a firstfruits observance," Karen explained. After placing a few samples of our produce in a bowl, we thank God, acknowledging that everything comes from Him. Then, silently, we each eat a portion. The simple tradition reminds us that God, too, must be first in our lives."

The Root of the Matter: Why not give structure and ceremony to your thankfulness? Life is filled with firstfruits—not just those from our gardens, but other important firsts—a first diploma, a first job, a first paycheck, a first house, a firstborn child. In each case, God is worthy of recognition and thanks, for whether we confess it or not, He deserves it the most.

The Fragrance of Praise: I thank You, dear God, for the sublime joy that accompanies every happy "first."

Garden Tools: As the growing season winds down, pluck extra blooms from your vegetable plants. These late blooms will not mature into produce, and removing the blooms will divert growth to already developing produce.

Wildflowers: Old English planting rhyme:
> *One to rot, and one to grow,*
> *One for the pigeon, one for the crow.*

Forever-greens

"Give, and it will be given to you."
LUKE 6:38 NIV

Upon Uncle Herman's invitation, newlyweds Linda and Henry Harder moved into the home of Henry's deceased grandmother. Herman insisted, "The house needs a family." Built on a cattle ranch, Grandma Frankie's dream house boasts maple floors, granite siding, and huge windows in view of rock outcroppings and pastureland. Linda even likes the 1950s wall colors. She feels honored to tread the well-worn Karastan carpets and live in a home with family history. But the most treasured household sentiment is a green memento that grows in the solarium.

GARDENING

Six months after Linda and Henry moved in, a neighbor rang the doorbell. "Hello, I'm an old friend of Frankie's." Erma held a shiny-leaf plant in a large coffee can. "I've had this for forty years. Frankie gave it to me and I thought it should come back to the family." Erma extended the *Hoya* plant as gently as she would handle a baby.

Linda was overwhelmed. "It was so heartwarming that with her fond attachment to Frankie, she was willing to give it up," she said. When Uncle Herman dropped by and heard the story, he, too, was pleased. He remembered well his mother's plant, especially its fragrant white clusters of waxy flowers.

But Erma's kindness didn't stop with Linda and Henry. Frankie's daughter, Christine, came to visit and was elated. She suggested that Linda give shoots of the plant to all the daughters, daughters-in-law, granddaughters, and granddaughters-in-law. "I decided I'd start snipping the shoots as soon as the next one appeared," said Linda, "so I'd have enough to give each one a potted start at Christmas."

By December, she had five small plants set in African violet pots Grandma Frankie had left in the basement. The red, blue, green, yellow, and black pots with wicks and drain dishes were just the right size for the young *Hoyas*. On Christmas morning, two generations of delighted recipients opened their gifts from the triple benefactors–Grandma Frankie, Erma, and Linda.

Christine says she feels a kinship with her mother each time she waters the plant. "The first year, it grew so slowly, I wondered if it would ever mature. Then one day I noticed a leafless shoot eighteen to twenty-four inches long. Gradually, joints appeared, and one by one, a dozen six-inch leaves unfurled along the length of the stem."

Linda hasn't taken her *Hoya* from the coffee can. "I keep it in a basket; I'm timid about doing anything more for it than watering and fertilizing. It's a precious possession I don't want to harm."

The day Grandma Frankie gave Erma the *Hoya,* she had no idea her gift would return to bless her offspring. But giving always pays a dividend.

The Root of the Matter: We never lose when we give, only when we hoard. Remember to give if you intend to gain. It's one of God's principles. Each glance at Grandma Frankie's *Hoya* plant reminds Linda that giving rebounds in a blessing.

The Fragrance of Praise: I am grateful and amazed, O God, at the ways You bless our giving with compensations that delight us.

Garden Tools: Certain species of *Hoya* prefer an acid soil mix. To start new plants, cut stems into one to two-inch lengths, with a single leaf and leaf axil bud. Insert into pots of cuttings soil mix and put in a propagator, keeping temperature at 59–64 degrees.

Wildflowers: "Generous people are rarely mentally ill."
DR. KARL MENNINGER

Small Beginnings

*"The people should not think
that small beginnings are unimportant."*
ZECHARIAH 4:10 NCV

Write a book on the subject of gardening? If someone had suggested such a project twenty-four years ago, I would have listened in disbelief. Then, I was neither author nor gardener.

We had just moved into our first house. Its sparse lawn was home to a thriving forsythia and a purple-blooming clematis. A few shasta daisies graced a south border, but nothing more than worms and weeds inhabited the other roughly edged beds. It was there I experienced my modest beginnings as a gardener.

My esthetic nature yearned for color, texture, and beauty in the yard. My early experimenting began with a few bare root roses. Though caring for our newborn, I found time to plant ponies of nonstop begonias and some petunias around the base of the clematis. They made a showy display through the kitchen window.

My plants became my tutors, and I enjoyed even the failures because I was learning. "Well, I guess I'll just cut this stem about here and move this plant over there." But guesses and hunches didn't pass with gardening, I discovered.

I began to glean expertise from experienced gardeners and became a faithful follower of planting and care instructions. I learned about zones (locales and climates that certain plants prefer), recommended exposures (shade or sun? morning or afternoon sun?), soil requirements (acidic or alkaline soil), vulnerability to disease (roses and fungi), and tolerance for frigid winters—all vital information paramount to the livelihood of my plant investments. And I dug in the dirt, watered, fertilized, harvested, and sweated a lot. Between times, I attended writers' conferences and collected a folder full of rejection slips. Yet slowly, more of my flowers flourished and more of my literary submissions sold.

I've grown as much as my garden—grown from the lessons that plant life has taught me. Among those principles is one best stated in the words I once saw stitched on a banner: "It takes a lot of SLOW, to grow." I've garnered knowledge and experience that now surprises me. I hear myself, the elder gardener, telling others what, where, and how about garden matters. But I always remember: My education came as slowly as the process from seed to seedling, from sapling to adult redwood.

The Root of the Matter: The most valuable lesson I've learned is that all things begin small. From infant to adult, from foundation to skyscraper, from novice to mentor. Never demean the small beginnings in any new endeavor. Tomorrow you may write a book on the topic that overwhelms you today!

The Fragrance of Praise: It feels good, God, to realize how far You've brought me and to know the distance ahead awaits with equal joy.

Garden Tools: Join a gardening book club. If you maintain

your membership for only one year, you'll acquire a few free books and low-cost additions that will answer many of your questions and afford you the convenience of handy reference.

Wildflowers: "My garden began with a package of catnip seeds a friend gave me to grow for my cat."

HARRIET CROSBY,
author of *A Well-Watered Garden*

Hope Pansies

And he himself has promised us this: eternal life.
1 JOHN 2:25 TLB

Writing a cheery garden book during our frigid Northwest winter felt as unfitting as imagining the warmth of summertime while grieving the death of a child. Such was my plight. My first grandchild passed away only weeks before, and now I was forced to settle into a writing discipline for a book-length manuscript. How would I do it? I could hardly compose a brief E-mail message. My emotions were raw with sorrow. The capacity for creative communication belonged to those people called authors, not me.

Among the sympathy cards sent to our family was a glossy note card of purple pansies. "Pansies are my flowers of hope," my friend had written. "They return every year, they survive our severe winter climate, they bloom long into the fall, and often endure even through the first month of winter. And they are beautiful, colorful, and lively. They sing to me of better days. . ."

Hope was the word that grabbed my heart. "Pansies are my flowers of hope." A pansy fancier myself, I always flanked my patio with a large basket of them. But I never thought of pansies as symbols of hope. For my friend, Roberta, their endurance through changing temperatures conveyed that message.

True, all hope for fulfillment of my plans with baby June was dashed. Yet over and over, the hope of heaven buoyed my sunken heart. Not a "hope-so" hope! Not an "if-there-is-a heaven" perspective. It was a fact in my soul; rooted deeper than pansies, far deeper than a ponderosa pine. The stabilizing factor through mournful days was the indisputable assurance of heaven where this grandmother and her firstborn grandchild would reunite. She was beyond the reach of my yearning arms, but hope for our future was certain.

Through those first shocking weeks of grief, the growing reality of that hope continued to steady me. Not only would our bereaved family survive our loss, but we could also look forward to seeing our little girl in yonder years.

Not aware of how gripped I was by her words, Roberta sent me a gift of pansies pressed between small glass panes and framed in pewter. Now hung from a silver cord in my kitchen window, it catches the light like that which brightens every eternal moment of my grandchild's new life. And yes, the pressed pansies "sing to me of better days" in heaven.

Thus, I began and completed this collection of garden essays comforted often by hope and have dedicated the whole to one precious pansy, my granddaughter, June Marie Joyce.

Tricolor pansies will always smile at me from beds, planters, and pots with a vibrant message—the hope of eons spent with God and kin.

The Root of the Matter: Death does not signal an end for those who have put their faith in Jesus Christ. Rather, it introduces a grand new beginning. Because Jesus Christ conquered death through His resurrection, believers will live with Him eternally. Though incomprehensible to us who are still earthbound, the glory that waits beyond death far surpasses the greatest glories of our mortal life.

The Fragrance of Praise: Dear God, I'm grateful for Your companionship in grief and the reality of Your comfort.

Garden Tools: Mingle pansies with chamomile. The faster growing chamomile will fill in around the long-stemmed pansies. The light green chamomile makes a lovely contrast for a pansy display. Shelter pansies from afternoon sun. Hybrid mixtures are recommended because they flower early and are heat-resistant.

Wildflowers: Pansies are from the genus *Viola*. Have you heard someone called "a shrinking violet"? The metaphor refers to a person who is painfully shy. More specifically, the expression is spoken of a pretty young girl who is retiring or bashful.

Bibliography

1001 Hints and Tips for Your Garden, Pleasantville, NY, Readers Digest Association, Inc., 1996.

A Well-Watered Garden, by Harriet Crosby, Nashville, Thomas Nelson, 1995.

Bartlett's Familiar Quotations, by John Bartlett, fifteenth edition. Boston: Little, Brown, and Co. 1980, 173.

Better Homes and Garden New Complete Guide to Gardening, by Susan A. Roth, Better Homes and Garden Books, Des Moines, 1997.

Compton's Encyclopedia On line web site: http://www.comptons.com/index_retail.html

Country Home, September/October 1997, 98, 102.

Flowers Are Forever, by Kathy Lamancusa, Simon & Schuster, New York, 2000.

Microsoft Encarta Encyclopedia CD, Microsoft Corporation, 1993–97.

Gardening for Dummies, 2nd Edition, 1999.

Gardening Notes and Quotes, Exley Publications, 1997.

Inheriting Paradise, Meditations on Gardening, by Vigen Guroian, Eerdmans, Grand Rapids, Mich. 1999.

New Choices, Rescuing Plants from the Past, *Reader's Digest,* March 2000 issue, 56–57.

Peter's Quotations, by Dr. Laurence J. Peter, Bantam Books, New York, 1977, 357.

Plants of the Bible, by Allan A. Swenson, Carol Publishing Group, New York, 1995.

Roses, A Celebration, by Rosamond Richardson, 1984, 36.

Souvenirs, Gifts from the Garden, by Kathryn Kleinman & Michaele Thunen, Hallmark Books, Collins Publishers, San Francisco, 1994.

Sunset Western Garden Book, by the editors of Sunset Books and Sunset Magazine, Sunset Publishing Corp., Menlo Park, CA, 1995 570, 520.

The American Horticultural Society Encyclopedia of Gardening, Christopher Brickell & Elvin McDonald, 1993.

The Dandelion Celebration: A Guide to Unexpected Cuisine, by Dr. Peter Gail, Goosefoot Acres Press, Cleveland, 1994.

The Gardener's Eye, by Allen Lacy, The Atlantic Monthly Press, NY, 1992.

The Heirloom Gardener, by Jo Ann Gardner, Storey Communications, Inc., Pownal, VT, 1992.

The Real Personages of Mother Goose, by Katherine Elwes Thomas, Lothrop, Lee, & Shepard Co., Boston, 1930, 8, 170.

The Spokesman-Review, 1999 *Home & Garden* article, "Gardens with Wings."

The Story of the Butchart Gardens, by Dave Preston, 1996, Highline Publishing, http://www.netbc.com.

Thoreau on Man and Nature, Peter Pauper Press, Inc., Mt. Vernon, NY, 1960.

Tussie-Mussies, by Geraldine Adamich Laufer, Workman Publishing, NY, 1993, 82.

About the Author

Niki **Anderson** is the author of the best-seller, *What My Cat Has Taught Me About Life.* She shares more lessons for living in this new collection of colorful metaphors from the garden.

Niki attended Northwest Nazarene College in Boise, Idaho; Elim Bible Institute in Lima, New York; and a Bible training fellowship in Port Arthur, Texas. She teaches writing classes at Spokane Falls Community College and also teaches at writers' conferences.

Her occupations have ranged from wife and mother, bookkeeper for two firms, missionary teacher in Africa, and pastor's secretary. She speaks to women's groups, at grade schools, and has led Bible studies and taught Sunday school to both adults and children.

As a freelance writer, Niki has received two Angel Awards for her devotional books for cat lovers, most recently for *Inspur-r-rational Stories for Cat Lovers.* She has written greeting card sentiments, interviews, personality profiles, and Sunday school take-home papers, and has been a contributor in five book compilations. Her articles have appeared in *Home Life, Decision, Aglow, Woman's*

Touch, The Upper Room, Herald of Holiness, and other publications. Niki is a member of the National League of American Pen Women.

To contact the author: Niki Anderson, P.O. Box 30222, Spokane, Washington 99223-3003

About the Editor

C **ristine Bolley,** editor for the new hobby series from Promise Press, is also an author and inspirational speaker. Her love for gardening sprouted during her childhood while decorating mud pies with flowers from her mother's garden. Visits to her grandmother's garden rooted her need to plant her own family legacy of love. Her three daughters and husband, James, all share her delight for sitting on their porch and watching their own garden grow. Her first illustrated children's book will be released in the fall of 2001, titled *A Gift from St. Nicholas.*

To contact the editor: Cristine Bolley, Wings Unlimited, P.O. Box 691532, Tulsa, OK 74169-1532